This book is dedicated to Emilie
(for sharing her love with me)

and to

for caring enough to read this book.

Chapter 1 : She'll Chew You Up.
Chapter 2 : The Moment I Knew.
Chapter 3 : My Last Two Bucks.
Chapter 4 : Guilty Pleasures.
Chapter 5 : Public Forum.
Chapter 6 : Gratitude.
Chapter 7 : City Living.
Chapter 8 : Trust 'Em Til Ya Bust 'Em.
Chapter 9 : Jungle Juicer.
Chapter 10 : Growth Spurt.
Chapter 11 : No Place Like 'Nome.
Chapter 12 : Mixtapes.
Chapter 13 : Respect Due.
Chapter 14 : A Bribe Called Request.
Chapter 15 : Ladies First?
Chapter 16 : Uncomfortably Numb.
Chapter 17 : The Price You Pay.
Chapter 18 : Le Freak. I Shreiked.
Chapter 19 : You Don't Say.
Chapter 20 : Ain't No Half Steppin'.
Chapter 21 : You're Killin' Me Smalls.
Chapter 22 : Thanks For The Memories.
Chapter 23 : Broken Hearted.
Chapter 24 : Reality Bites.
Chapter 25 : Do-It-Yourself Project.
Chapter 26 : Momma's Boy.
Chapter 27 : Short Cuts.
Chapter 28 : Closing Time.
Chapter 29 : My Final Stand.
Chapter 30 : Never Tear Us Apart.

Foreword

My name is Craig, and I am a DJ and the originator of Retronome – a throwback dance party that began in 1996 at Club Metronome in Burlington, Vermont. I have also been a close friend of Kyle, the author of this book, for more than 20 years.

In 1999, after a six-week stint spinning in Jamaica for Spring Break, I was preparing to move to the New York City area. It was time to pass on my baby, *Retronome*, to another DJ. I considered a few from the area, but Kyle was the only one stupid enough to accept the gig.

> *I mean, I tried to warn him... people can be so fucking rude when requesting songs from us. IT'S A SONG PEOPLE! REALLY? From drinks being thrown in your face to name calling, we deal with it all.*

So who better to take this all on than Kyle, whom I'd worked with as a regular guest with his traveling firestorm band, *Belizbeha*.

Kyle is not only a music lover, he is the ULTIMATE music control freak. For example, he recorded a stack of CD's with my playlist written on them and asked that I NOT bring any music with me when I was the DJ at his wedding reception!

I knew that he'd be able to hold his own with the regulars that descended upon Club Metronome weekly. His DJ skills were still developing in the early stages, but he was definitely the man to make sure that everything was perfect, regardless of the task at hand. I also appreciated, and was very familiar with, his wit and sense of humor. I knew that he would use it to stock an arsenal of responses to combat testy requesters in any situation.

Over the years, he's grown into a true DJ; one that everyone respects, not only for his mixing skills, but, also for his *ear*. He's the guy finding the bootleg remixes of everything under the sun and isn't afraid to LOU RAWLS you right off the bat. With a nod to the past and a foot in the future, the true artist in him paints musical pictures that truly take you on a journey. And that's what he does in the pages of this book – paints pictures.

So strap in for the ride folks. I know you're going to enjoy these stories as much as he (and I) have while experiencing them live.

Sometimes, you have to suffer for your art...other times, you're tortured.

Enjoy the tales within.

(P.S. Kyle was the only person I asked to take over for me...my first and only choice.)

Sincerely,

Craig Mitchell,
DJ, music lover and life coach

Introduction

Once upon a time...

... I was a 400-pound '80s DJ.

Hello. My name is Martin Kyle Thompson.
Or, as some people may know me, DJ Fattie B.

For the past 16-plus years, I have worked every Saturday night as the DJ at a dance club in Burlington, Vermont, called Club Metronome. The club is at 188 Main Street, in the heart of a hopping college-town bar scene. Although these weekly parties (billed as "Retronome") that have been my bread and butter also include some '70s music, the nights are throwback events focusing on the dance songs of the 1980s.

Being in my forties, I came of age during this period and, subsequently, have many nostalgic memories connected to these songs. I graduated from high school in 1988, so my developmental years *were* the mid-'80s. This era's songs remind me of dances, girlfriends, parties, sports events and so on. However, my experiences of the last decade and a half as an '80s-night DJ have made these songs soundtracks for a whole new set of memories.

These memories are why you and I find ourselves intersecting here and now. While most people think that a DJ's life is all *hands in the air* and VIP parties (and believe me, some nights it is), I've written this book to expose the underbelly, to revel in — and laugh about — the uglier truths of being a small-town DJ.

The following is a collection of stories and reminiscences shared through the music of the '80s. Each chapter begins with the lyrics of a song that captures, for me, the musical essence of each individual message.

A few warnings: Some of the language contained in these pages may be a bit *spicy*. Some of the things I share in here are just fantasies (and/or daydreams) and not anything I would ever *actually do* for real. Some of the stories may seem too outrageous to possibly be true. I promise you: They are all 98.5% accurate.

And, just in case you think you may have been at the club while I was spinning, fear not: The names have been changed to protect the guilty.

Well, then - I've been told the only way to really go swimming is to dive right in, so... allow me to start with a cannonball.

SHE'LL CHEW YOU UP.

"She'll only come out at nights
The lean and hungry type
Nothing is new
I've seen her here before
Watching and waiting
Ooh, she's sittin' with you
But her eyes are on the door
(Oh-oh, here she comes)
Watch out boy, she'll chew you up
(Oh-oh, here she comes)
She's a maneater"

Maneater by Hall & Oates
Written by Sara Allen, Darryl Hall & John Oates
Released in 1982 by RCA

For the first 10 years of my residency at Club Metronome in Burlington, Vermont, my DJ booth was a small room behind the stage, which was also home to the band green room and numerous beer coolers.

The booth was about 8 feet by 6 feet and housed the club's entire sound system of amplifiers, making it unbearably cramped and hot. In the summertime, it was a virtual sauna. It was also about 3 feet away from the employee restroom, so, when a 350-pound bouncer dropped his kids off at the pool, the smell found its way directly to my nose. Other odors of my work environment included warm, stale beer and the faint but permanent smell of vomit. When I DJ'd, a 2 foot by 3 foot peephole directly in front of me allowed me a limited view onto the dancefloor.

One hot summer night, I had a moment between song mixes and stepped out of my sweaty booth to find one of the club's bouncers searching the backstage area. He asked me if I had seen an "extremely wasted woman in her 70s" come through the back. The missing granny was a regular drunk we all knew (and of whom we were more than wary). I told him that I had yet to see her that night but that I would keep my eyes peeled.

A few songs later, I heard a loud groan from the green room next to my booth. My first thought was, *Oh, no, she must have fallen down.*

I stepped out to find the green-room door closed. I turned the handle and pushed on the door, but it was blocked by something (or *someone*). I leaned my shoulder into it and forced the door open to reveal a sight that, unfortunately,

I can never unsee: A 22- to 25-year-old pale, freckled, nerdy ginger standing facing me and the missing elderly lady down on her knees in front of him — his penis balls deep in her mouth.

I stared, frozen and amazed by this morally questionable union but was more surprised by the vision above the back of her half-balding, gray-haired head. As my eyes slowly scanned upward (and desperately tried to pull away from the car wreck of a blowjob happening in front of me), I witnessed the nerd smiling from ear to ear like he had just won the lottery. His left hand gave me a super enthusiastic thumbs-up while his right hand proudly displayed his trophy:

the grandma's dentures!

I swear to the good Lord above.

I started to reach out to tap her on the shoulder to break it up and let them both know that they had to get out of there, but paused ... and gently closed the door. It simply wasn't my place to interrupt this love connection. When they had finished, the Opie look-a-like dipped his head into my booth and dropped a $10 bill on my mixer.

"Thanks for lettin' her finish, bud," his creepy voice whispered in my ear.

I never felt good about that tip, but probably better than he did about the *tip* he gave her that night.

                Then I wondered,

        in that odd moment on that odd night,

            How the hell did I get here?

THE MOMENT I KNEW.

*"Hey, listen up to your local deejay
You better hear what he's got to say*

*There's not a problem that I can't fix,
'cause I can do it in the mix*

*Last night a deejay saved my life
Last night a deejay saved my life from a broken heart
Last night a deejay saved my life
Last night a deejay saved my life with a song"*

Last Night A DJ Saved My Life by Indeep
Written by Michael Cleveland
Released in 1982 by Sound Of New York

How does a kid from a tiny, rural northeastern town like Bristol, Vermont, find his way to becoming a DJ?

Growing up in a place that was only 40 square miles and had a population of about 2,000 in the early '80s made me be nothing else if not *creative*. I was also an artistic soul, so I learned a way to make anything fun and created games that challenged my abilities.

Bristol was — and, in many ways, still is — a Hallmark-esque interpretation of strong community and serenity, but there's not much to do in a town 40 to 50 miles from any real *activity*. To this day, Bristol's main claim to fame is the annual 4th of July Outhouse Races up and down Main Street. It's pretty self-explanatory: Locals build outhouses on wheels and race them around the town green. #truestory.

The town is so small that, to make a respectable high school, four other similarly-sized towns had to join together and form Mouth Abraham Union High School. Seriously.

How I became a teenage rap fiend there I couldn't really say. However, as is the case with anyone's life, there are specific moments that occur that shape you and send you on the path to your destiny. How I found *my way* to music (or more accurately, how music *found* me) was developed through four noteworthy experiences:

1. 1978. I am 8 years old.

My sister Stephanie and her friend Anne (who lived with us for a short time that year) were typical high schoolers of the era and loved to play their favorite records as loudly as possible ad nauseum. There was one particular record that struck multiple chords within my creative soul: *A Night At The Opera* by Queen. The music was unlike anything else being played on the radio at the time and was so powerful it stayed with you far beyond your listening session. And, as the yet undiscovered artistic side of me was being born, my mind's eye still holds a clear image of the record's amazing cover art. This was the first time I began to meld art and music as one, and it changed me forever.

2. 1981. I am now 11.

Soon after I got my first radio boombox, I began to collect my favorite songs by listening to radio personality Casey Kasem's *America's Top 40* on Saturdays and recording them on the unit's cassette recorder. This also was the era of *Solid Gold*, the TV show that featured dancers performing borderline risque dances to the week's top 10 hits. The combination of these two phenomena sparked my interest in popular music and a yearning to *perform*.

Inevitably, I formed a "band" of lip synchers (with my little brother, Chris, my friend Sal who lived down the street, and my cousin Brian). We compiled our favorite songs of the time from my cassette recordings, made a set list, and invited our families to my house for a Sunday afternoon concert. We used buckets and a laundry basket for drums, tennis rackets as our guitars and bass, and my dad's screwdrivers and flashlights for microphones. As our parents and siblings sat in our basement and acted entertained, I noticed their attention drifting by the third song. I panicked and, desperate for this show to be a success, began to spaz out on the drums in an attempt to make people laugh. My bandmates weren't impressed, but in my mind I saved the gig from disaster. This was when I experienced my first pangs of hunger for that *in-the-spotlight* feeling.

3. 1986. I am now 16 and driving.

We grew up on the town line and were surrounded by mountains that blocked our cable TV reception. I remember being mad at *those frickin' mountains* and wishing we'd move just to be able to have cable TV like other normal teenagers. And one of the main reasons I yearned for it was *Yo! MTV Raps*. The new MTV series highlighting rap stars and their videos was all I wanted to watch.

Fortunately, I had a buddy who lived in the village, in a house that did have cable and MTV. So I made the deal of my young lifetime with him: He'd record *Yo!* on VHS for me and, in exchange, I'd give him rides to and from school every day. Monday mornings consisted of my leaving an hour early for school and watching the tape in his living room while he and his family ate their breakfast in their kitchen. My obsession with rap (and its culture) began to grow out of control. In a town teeming with Billy Idol and Bon Jovi fans, I had to develop thick skin, since many other kids were rude to me for choosing to listen to the likes of Big Daddy Kane and Doug E. Fresh.

But I honestly couldn't help myself: Rap music struck a chord within my soul.

It was an itch that had to be *scratched*.

4. **Jump back to 1983. My very first junior high dance.**

Mt. Abraham Union High School gymnasium in Bristol.

As I pushed open the double doors and made my way through the maze of 200 or so students inside the gym, my eyes grew wide as I saw *them*.

In the far corner under the basketball hoop, moving in total unison, *they* were a group of three similarly dressed high school students known as the Electric Shuttle Crew.

They had headbands, wristbands, and gold chains.
They were the freshest.
The dopest.
The coolest.
And they were at *our* school!
They were break dancers.

My jaw dropped. I was absolutely hypnotized and paralyzed by their moves and, more importantly, by the power of the music that guided their flow. And whether it was fate, or just dumb luck, the song quoted at the start of this chapter was pumping through the super-sized sound system brought in by the person in charge of this musical gathering: the DJ. I remember it was loud, it was mesmerizing, and it was the coolest thing I had ever seen. The three breakers popped and locked, surging the energy of the crowd with every new dance move. When the DJ mixed in "Rockit" by Herbie Hancock and the head spins began, something changed inside me. With every scream from the crowd, the truth of that moment grew clearer to me: I knew that I wanted to be the person who controlled the crowd and brought the people joy.

I wanted to be the one to share the emotions and feelings that I was experiencing at that exact moment with others.

There was no question whatsoever:

I would do whatever it took to become a DJ.

MY LAST TWO BUCKS.

"When I wake up people take up mostly all of my time
I'm not singin', phone keep ringin' cause I make up a rhyme
I'm not braggin', people naggin' cause they think I'm a star
Always tearin' what I'm wearin', I think they're goin' too far..."

It's Tricky by Run-DMC
Written by Joseph Simmons, Darryl McDaniels, Doug Fieger, Berton Averre
Released in 1986 on Profile

It's now 1986. At this point I'm 16 and have been a DJ for about a year. My equipment setup is the stuff of lawn sale legends: one belt-drive turntable, a five disc CD changer, and one dual-cassette player. My mixer is a Gemini three-channel beauty that my brother and I had bought with money we earned mowing lawns that summer.

Side DJ nerd-out note: This mixer was purchased out of the J&R World catalog that came to our house every few months. The days the catalogs arrived in our mailbox were like Christmas for my brother and me, as we turned each page and dreamed of all the amazing equipment we wanted but never had the money to actually buy. Someday, we pined ...

Besides local DJ, the other important title I held at this point in my young life now was "licensed driver." My car was a dusty blue Ford Fairmont station wagon. She was far from sexy but had earned a nickname equivalent to a promiscuous Purple Heart: the "Shaggin' Wagon."

I remember hooking up two massive home stereo speakers to the car's speaker wires and just laying them in the back. They were loud as hell but, in all honesty, never quite bumped enough for my liking. Anytime my friends and I wanted to party in the woods (as any self-respecting Vermont kid knows well), I could just open the hatch back, drag them out and, *voila*: instant mobile sound system.

One Saturday afternoon, through a series of testosterone-filled phone calls, I helped organize a party for later that night to be set up in the field behind my buddy's house.

With a barn nearby, I was going to have a power supply for my DJ gear. I began eagerly organizing my music for the kegger: three crates of records to the left, a shoebox of cassettes to the right, and a giant suitcase of CDs. As I plotted my set list,
a pretty young lady in whom I had a very serious interest in groping called to make sure that I had *all* of her favorite music ready to go:

        Prince — Check.
    Michael Jackson — Check.
  Beastie Boys — Oh, hell to the yes.

Then she said it: "It's Tricky" by Run-DMC.

I knew this song and loved it, but I'd yet to actually purchase my own copy. This is 1986 now — you can't just download it or play it on YouTube. You had to go to the music store and actually *buy it*.

And all I wanted to do was make her happy, because, if she was happy, then there was a solid chance that I would be happ*ier*. So I ran out and jumped in my car to make the 35-minute drive to the Strawberries record store on Shelburne Road.

About 20 minutes into my journey, I glance down at my dashboard and noticed that I was running very low on gas. I fumbled for my Swatch wallet and opened it to discover two single dollar bills and a crusty condom. I had pushed the boundaries of my gas tank's depths before and, being more than halfway there, I simply said, *Fuck it* and decided to go for broke.

I arrived at the store and found the "It's Tricky" cassingle, which is what cassette singles were called back in the day. They went for $1.88 (with tax). I excitedly handed over my last two dollars and literally skipped my way through the lot back to my car. I peeled off the plastic and slid the tape into the stereo. The B-side was "Proud To Be Black," which I also loved, so I just played one side and then the other, one side and then the other, over and over, pretending that I was *in* Run-DMC.

About 8 miles from home, my car began to sputter. A few heartbreaking seconds later, I had no choice but to ease her to a slow, rolling stop on the roadside. I was completely out of gas. Bone-dry empty. I had no cell phone - it's 1986, remember - and no way to call for help. But I really didn't give a shit. All that mattered to the then 16-year-old version of myself was that *I had the song.*

Eventually, I figured, a car would come driving along and I would just flag them down for a ride.

So, until someone pulled over, I just smiled and hit play...

"This beat is my recital..."

GUILTY PLEASURES.

"Well, I was there and I saw what you did
I saw it with my own two eyes
So you can wipe off that grin,
I know where you've been
It's all been a pack of lies

I can feel it coming in the air tonight,
oh Lord
& I've been waiting for this moment for all my life, Oh Lord
Can you feel it coming in the air tonight?
Oh Lord, Oh Lord"

In The Air Tonight by Phil Collins
Written by Phil Collins
Released in 1981 on Virgin, Atlantic

Fall of '86.

Feeling confident in my musical endeavors and with my parents out of town for the night, I decided to set up my DJ equipment and host a small party in the basement of our home. I decorated with red lights and strobes, covered all the windows, and concealed the furnace and washer and dryer to transform the space into a no-fail makeout den. Then I invited six of the cutest girls from school and three of my guy friends (to ensure the odds were tilted in our favor).

The ladies were greeted by four super-horny teenage guys and a metal tub filled with ice-cold Bartles & James Strawberry Kiwi wine coolers. The party was also well stocked with Doritos, lip balm and the unmistakable scent of Old Spice cologne. We jammed to some rap and R&B hits, and then I smoothly transitioned into a mixtape that I'd titled *THE MAKEOUT MASTER*. It had some Al B. Sure, some Prince, a little Journey, Foreigner, Hall & Oates, and just a smidge of Richard Marx.

Obviously, my mixtapes' power was irresistible: We began to couple off and spread out like a recon mission. One couple on the loveseat. Another on the bench in the corner. Trying to find some semblance of privacy, my cutie and I walked upstairs and wandered outside to our backyard. We ended up standing face-to-face behind the small shed my dad had built to store our lawn tools and mower.

Now, up to this point, this girl and I had only kissed once (about a week prior). So, although we were both nervous, I knew it was going down. And then... *she went down*. She unzipped my parachute pants and pulled out my diamond-cutter-of-a boner. She slowly stroked me as I closed my eyes and tipped my head back, anticipating the soon-to-be-on-me feel of her mouth. As I stood there, eyes closed, I felt a distinct *chill*. A *presence*. Like someone was ... watching. I hesitantly opened my left eye to see, standing behind my date and staring directly at me with a fierce and potent cocktail of anger and utter disbelief, the *one* person you would *never, ever* want to see at that exact moment:

My Momma.

She had returned from her trip surprisingly early.

The silence was deafening.

No one uttered a word. My mother just stood there, her glare so intense that, I swear, disappointment lasers shot out of her eyes and pierced my soul. I wanted to look away (but was frozen in place like Han Solo) and was unable to do anything but defenselessly stare back. Her scalding and scolding eyes spoke volumes to me in that next 20 seconds (which felt much more like 20 minutes).

And then, as quickly as she had appeared, my mother turned and walked away without saying a word. Unbelievably, my partner in Dirty Town hadn't noticed (or stopped). In fact, she never even knew my mom had been there at all.

But I knew.

And, consequently, I almost couldn't come due to the weight of the guilt that had now been cloaked upon me.

Almost.

But fortunately, reality set in: I remembered that I was a 16-year-old boy, and pretty soon I came like a Civil War cannon.

My mother and I never spoke about that incident. But my punishment was (and still is) the eternal memory of *her glare*.

To this very day, I still shiver whenever thinking about it.

PUBLIC FORUM.

"There's things that you guess
And things that you know
There's boys you can trust
And girls that you don't
There's little things you hide
And little things that you show
Sometimes you think you're gonna get it
But you don't and that's just the way it goes

It's natural
It's chemical (let's do it)
It's logical
Habitual (can we do it?)
It's sensual
But most of all...
Sex is something we should do
Sex is something for me and you"

I Want Your Sex by George Michael
Written by George Michael
Released in 1987 on Epic

The crowds that have filled Club Metronome over the years can be described as eclectic at best. Young and old, well-off and poor, educated and red-necked. All races, all types. But one common objective (beyond dancing) that brings the people out is everyone's favorite three-letter word: sex. People like it, yearn for it, and, apparently, will consume great quantities of alcohol to *help* find it and/or make it happen.

As I stated previously, for the first 10 years or so of my time at Retronome, I DJ'd from inside a small room behind the stage that had a small peephole through which I could see the dance floor. There were, however, two problems with this viewpoint:

1. Because people were dancing on an elevated stage, my view through this hole was from their shoulders down to their knees. If I wanted to see someone's face or speak with them, either I had to duck down and look up or they had to bend over and look down.

2. When the club was packed and the stage was full, my view of the dance floor was completely blocked.

One particularly hot midsummer night, the club was absolutely slammed. Capacity was 262, and we were at about 305. Shoulder to shoulder and a straight sweat box.

I had a friend from out of town visiting and hanging in the booth with me. He was intrigued by the scene unfolding in front of him, and what happened next made his visit even more unforgettable.

Directly in front of my window, a young couple was intertwined in a serious grinding session. She stood in front of him, wearing a much-too-small tank top, a smaller mini skirt, and Jersey Shore levels of mascara. He was positioned behind her, gripping her hips while he pushed up into her backside with his liquor-induced chubby. As I faded in the 12" dance remix of "Relax" by Frankie Goes To Hollywood, she effortlessly reached back and flipped up her mini skirt. She then rolled her thong down under her ass cheeks. Without missing a beat (or looking around at all), she reached behind herself to unzip his shorts, unleash his boner, and slide it inside her. (Reminder: It's shoulder-to-shoulder packed that night). My friend and I stood there amazed by the absence of shame in this wasted couple's *game*.

As I realized their thrusts were syncing up to the tempo of the song, I began to conduct an experiment. I began to slow the song down, and, as I did, they began to fuck ever more slowly. I then sped the beat back up and watched them simultaneously pick up their pace. My friend and I laughed until we cried as I flipped the fader from slow to fast and back again.

As the song ended and I transitioned into the next, I reached out my window and tapped the dude on the leg. "You've got one more song to finish up," I mouthed to him. He smiled as he nodded approvingly and began to thump-hump her like a rabbit just released from prison.

We watched him arch his back and give her one last deep, elongated thrust. He then slipped it out, tucked it away and zipped up. He turned to reach his arm into my window and, in a gesture of thanks, tried to fist bump me. Worried about the very real possibility of getting some of what he had just ejaculated on me, I denied the return bump and offered a friendly wave. We then watched him jump off the stage and scurry out the front door.

A few moments later the young lady involved leaned in my window and shyly asked me the following:

"Hey there. I saw you talking to that guy I was, um, *dancing* with... Do you know his name?"

GRATITUDE.

"I will have you
Yes, I will have you
I will find a way
and I will have you
Like a butterfly
A wild butterly
I will collect you and capture you"

Obsession by Animotion
Written by Holly Knight, Michael Des Barres
Released in 1984 on Mercury

Summer of 1987.

Before the dance club that I have DJ'd at for many years became Club Metronome, it was known as Border. And during the summer months of my teen years, Border was the nightspot of choice for area adolescents. Mondays and Tuesdays were teen nights known as The Young & The Restless dance parties. The DJ for these gatherings was the local legend Tod Warner (aka God Warner).

As a now 17-year-old, I went there first and foremost looking for girls, but, as an aspiring fellow DJ, I found myself becoming obsessed with the music Tod was introducing us all to. His record collection was insanely massive and his eclectic 12" remixes made the selector in me *cream*. I would try to not be a complete annoyance to him, but all too often I found myself standing at his window begging for the names of song artists and titles with every every record he spun.

When I would hear a remix that I had never heard before and witnessed the dance floor reaction to it, I would become *obsessed*. I *had* to have it. It was the same feeling I had when I was 9 and someone showed me a baseball card that didn't yet live in my own personal collection. I would hunt it down and capture it. I would become completely focused on one mission:
It would be *mine*.

After numerous trips to interrupt and question Tod, he finally turned and broke it down to me.

"Listen, kid," he calmly stated, "I appreciate your thirst for knowledge, but I'm spinning here. If you really want to talk records, I pick up my equipment at 4 p.m. here tomorrow. Come by then and we can chop it up. Cool?"

I nodded, shuffled away, and, for the rest of the night, left him alone.

But, sure as shit, I promptly pulled up to the club the next day at 3:54 p.m. with pen and pad in hand.

Throughout the next year, Tod and I spent numerous afternoons together talking music. Old music, new music, how to read a crowd, when to mix, what to mix, and how to let the DJ do his thing and avoid (at all costs) interrupting his flow. His words and knowledge helped shaped me as a DJ. His friendship helped shape me as a man.

I've never had the right chance to say these words until now, but I've always felt them:

Thank you, Tod.

CITY LIVING.

*"Got nothing against a big town
Still hayseed enough to say look who's in the big town
But my bed is in a small town
Oh, and that's good enough for me*

*Well I was born in a small town
And I can breathe in a small town
Gonna die in this small town
And that's prob'ly where they'll bury me"*

Small Town by John Cougar Mellencamp
Written by John Cougar Mellencamp
Released in 1985 on Riva Records

After high school, I moved 40 miles north to Burlington, Vermont. Burlington is the largest city in the state but is basically an overgrown town and an interesting (and maddening) dichotomy.

With a population of just under 50,000 and four colleges within a 10-mile radius, it is on one hand a picturesque lakeside Norman Rockwellian illustration of typical New England beauty.

However, when flipped over, its underbelly reveals a noisy, financially challenged and drug-ridden college constituency struggling with crime and mental illness issues often associated with much larger cities. Its geographic location as a connecting point to three larger cities (Montreal, Boston, and New York City) make it an intriguing destination to developers, touring bands, and drug dealers alike.

The number of "Best" and "Top 10, Top 50, and Top 100" lists that the city, its charming downtown and the local university have all made over the last decade alone perfectly illustrate these disparities:

2015: University of Vermont (UVM) ranked 85th in list of Best Colleges/National Universities

August 2014: UVM listed #18 among "Top 20 Party Schools" by Princeton Review

August 2013: Burlington ranked #2 among "America's 10 Great Places to Live" by *Kiplinger's Personal Finance*

2013: Burlington ranked #3 on list of "25 Most Hung Over Cities in America" by *Business Insider*

2012: Vermont (as a state) was ranked #5 on list of "America's Happiest States" by Gallup-Healthways Well-Being Index

August 2012: UVM ranked #19 among "Top 20 Party Schools" by Princeton Review

2012: Burlington ranked #23 on list of "Best College Towns in America" by bestcollegereviews.org

2012: Burlington ranked #25 among "The Top 25 Drunkest Cities" by *The Daily Beast*

2012: Burlington ranked #15 on list of "Best Cities to Meet Eligible Women" by *Men's Health*

2011: Burlington ranked #28 among "Worst Dressed Cities in America" list by *GQ Magazine*

2011: UVM ranked #14 on list of "Up-and-Coming Schools" by *U.S. News & World Report*

2011: UVM ranked #11 on "Top Party Schools" list by *Newsweek* and *The Daily Beast*

2010: Burlington named a "Top 10 City for the Next Decade" by *Kiplinger's Personal Finance*

2008: Burlington ranked 4th among "Top 10 Cities for Beer Lovers" by ShermansTravels.com

How does this city (and university) live such a double life?

How can an area have such an inebriated downtown population on a warm spring Saturday night yet 4,000 to 5,000 people running a marathon early Sunday morning? That's the mystery of it all.

One of my former coworkers at the club (after about five years' living in the city's downtown) once explained the psychological impact that this dual-personality environment can have on someone who is easily persuaded or distracted by social landscape:

> "Life here in Burlington, Vermont, is literally the period of life between high school and college.
>
> For most, that period lasts the length of a summer season and is typically a nostalgic last gasp of suspended maturation before the first chapter of *real life* truly begins.
>
> Here in Burlington, it's basically Groundhog Day.
>
> Same shit, different day.
> Wash, rinse, repeat.
>
> It never ends."

This is the city where I live and proudly DJ for its fine residents and tourists every single weekend.

        Rain, shine, sleet, snow, drunk, sober,
            happy, sad, or indifferent.

You can count on three things here: death, taxes, and good ol' Fattie B. spinning '80s music on Saturday nights.

I love my city and hope I have helped to keep the visitors and natives alike grooving.

Someone once asked me to describe Burlington.
I paused for a second, then remembered the wise words of a (drunken) college-age woman I overheard chatting with a friend late one night:

        "Burlington:
It's a quaint drinking village
with a small college problem".

TRUST 'EM TIL YA BUST 'EM.

"Now here you are begging to me
To give our love another try
Girl I love you and I always will
But darling right now I've got to say goodbye   'cause

I saw you (and him)
Standing in the rain
You were holding hands and I'll never be the same"

The Rain by Oran "Juice" Jones
Written by Vincent Bell
Released in 1986 on Def Jam

Infidelity: It's only cheating if you get caught. As unfortunate as this statement sounds, it seems to be the belief of many in today's world.

Pop singer Alanis Morrisette once famously quipped "You can't do monogamy 90 percent of the time." And one rainy summers night, I watched this play out in front of me at Metronome.

It was a typically busy Retronome. Around ten o'clock I noticed a young couple (seemingly in love) oogling over each other at the bar. They held hands, tracing each other's fingers, kissing gently as they stared into each other's eyes. About 45 minutes later, as I approached the bar to grab a beverage, I noticed the boyfriend saying goodbye and telling his girl to "Be good." He made his way towards the exit, but not before looking back three times and blowing her a kiss from afar.

Soon thereafter, a tall thin gentleman with a thick mustache and thicker French-Canadien accent (who had been requesting songs earlier) began to dance with the young lady who was now alone. She played shy at first, but the combined powers of his 'stache, his accent, his low cut V-neck t-shirt, and his heavily applied Georgio Armani cologne proved irresistible. Soon they were in full grind mode, doing what the kids like to call *dry humping*. He swung her around to face him and they embraced in a long and passionate kiss that made me wonder if she even remembered her recently absent boyfriend's name.

Then, when I was sure they couldn't have taken it any further in this most public of venues, he slid his hand down her back, up under her dress and beneath the edge of her panties — in a direct line to her butt crack. I can't be certain, but, from my view and the placement of his little French fingers, I'm 99 percent sure he popped his middle finger directly into her poop hole.

The Frenchie kept it there for a good minute.
And she rather liked it.

As I tapped one of the bouncers on the shoulder to point this out and explain the whole scenario to him, the story took a turn down soap opera avenue. Out of the corner of my eye, I noticed a dude standing off to the side and just staring at them both from the shadows.

It was her boyfriend. Unbeknownst to her and her new *friend,* he had returned and was watching it all unfold.

As the couple continued to make out and thrust, I mean dance, the boyfriend just sat and observed. He didn't show any emotions at all. He just stared and took mental notes. After approximately 30 to 40 minutes, he stood up, took a deep breath, and exhaled. I fully expected him to gather his anger, rush over, and confront this Romeo and his lady, but instead he turned and left. She never had any idea he had even come back and witnessed her cheating ways.

I wondered to myself, what was the conversation like when she next saw him face to face? I imagined it to be like Oran "Juice" Jones talking to his cheating woman at the end of the song "The Rain" from 1986. If you don't know the song, look it up and listen to it as you join me in imagining it going a little something like this:

"How was your day today? Did you miss me?

You did? Yeah? I missed you too.
I missed you so much, I followed you today.
That's right now close your mouth,
'cause you cold busted!

Now just sit down here, sit down here ...
I'm so upset with you I don't know what to do.

You know my first impulse was to run up on you and do a Rambo. I was about to jam you and flat blast both of you. But instead ... I chilled — that's right *chilled*.

I called up the bank and took out every dime.
Then I cancelled all your credit cards.

Don't go lookin' in that closet 'cause everything you came here with is packed up and waiting for you.

What were you thinking? I gave you things you couldn't even pronounce! But now I can't give you nothing but advice.

'Cause you're still young, yeah, you're young. And you're gonna find somebody like me one of these days ... Until then, know what you gotta do?

You gotta get on outta here with that alley-cat, hush puppy shoe wearing crumbcake I watched you with... 'cause you dismissed!

That's right, silly rabbit, tricks are made for kids, don't you know that? You without me is like corn flakes without the milk! This is my world! You're just a squirrel trying to get a nut!

Now get on outta here ...   Scat!"

JUNGLE JUICER.

*"This brother told me a secret
on how to get more chicks
Put a little Medina in ya glass
And the girl's will come real quick
It's better than any alcohol or ahprodisiac
A couple sips of this love potion
And she'll be on your lap*

*I asked the guy 'Why you so fly?'
He said Funky Cold Medina"*

Funky Cold Medina by Tone Loc
Written by Young MC, Michael Ross, Matt Dike
Released in 1989 on Delicious Vinyl

It's 1990. My first semester at Burlington's junior varsity higher learning institution, Champlain College.

I remember it was late fall and the first really cold night. I was about to DJ my first college house party, and I couldn't have been more excited. By this point, I was spinning with two Pioneer home stereo CD players and a (dope?) Radio Shack mixer. I remember this is when I started burning two copies of each disc so I could flip doubles back and forth.

I had all the jams ready to go: The hotness at the time was Digital Underground's "Humpty Dance," Bel Biv Devoe's "Do Me" and "Poison," and any C + C Music Factory track. My job was to make the ladies dance. When they danced, they got thirsty. When they got thirsty, they would want to drink. And my buddies (who were hosting this party) had the 'drink' situation on lock. You see, I was about to get my first taste of *jungle juice*.

Jungle juice, as I came to find out, was a large batch of punch made with various juices and flavored drinks used to hide the taste of the active ingredient: grain alcohol. Even though I was from the sticks in Vermont, I had never really known what grain alcohol was before this. As we mixed the party's signature concoction in their bathtub, my buddies broke it down for me: First, the grains are fermented to reach a high ethanol content. Then distillation produces a colorless yet crazy potent liquor. Because of its power (190 proof), grain alcohol should never be consumed straight. Thus, the juice gets you loose.

I remember few images from that night. One flash is of a packed dance floor and everyone happily getting down. Another is of me taking huge gulps of the juice out of a big-ass red tumbler. The next is of me macking on a chubby girl with braces near the back bathroom. And then (thankfully)... it's all just black.

Flash forward to some point later on:

As I'm coming back to reality, I'm confused, and my eyes are closed. The only thing I know for sure (as the fog in my skull begins to lighten) is that the right side of my face is really fucking cold. My chin, cheek, and temple are literally frozen. I slowly open my right eye I see a line of yellow dashes extending from the center of my eyeball outward. As I float back down to the earth's atmosphere, I open my left eye and begin to fully comprehend my current scenario: I'm lying in the middle of the street, with my head dead-center on the dotted yellow line that separates the lanes. I've somehow (quite mysteriously) stumbled away from the party, fallen into the road, and passed out right smack in the middle of it. Feeling lucky that my head wasn't run over or that I haven't been robbed or sent to detox, I sit up and scour the area for clues. An old, bent street sign lets me know that I'm about halfway between the party and my dorm.

As I made my way home, I was grateful for my safety. My good luck allowed me to survive that time unscathed. Moving forward, I used that experience to learn a valuable life lesson: It's okay to get drunk every once in a while, but know when enough is enough.

Also, as my good friend Timmer once summed up (perfectly, simply, and wisely):

"Moral of the story: Alcohol is *not* a toy".

To this very day, I have lived — and partied — by those sage words.

No more blackouts, Ma!

GROWTH SPURT.

"*Big time, I'm on my way I'm making it
Big time, oh yes
Big time, I've got to make it show yeah, Big time
Big time, so much larger than life
Big time, I'm gonna watch it **growing**,
Big time*"

Big Time by Peter Gabriel
Written by Peter Gabriel
Released in 1986 on Virgin

Throughout high school I was always active and involved in sports. However, as I began college and started to party more (and move less), I began to put on weight quickly. My family members are all larger in size. Growing up, we hardly ever experienced a shortage of butter or cheese in our family meals. And in what comes as a shock to no one who has ever known me, I have enjoyed smoking a little pot every now and then.

Let me tell ya, kiddos, pot equals two things:

1. A lot less athletic activity, and...
2. A lot more unhealthy eating habits.

In the early '90s, I began a period as a rapper for an acid-jazz band called Belizbeha. By this time I weighed more than 300 pounds (and was still gaining). I wanted an emcee name that represented my size and verbal dexterity on the mic. I remember being baked at a friend's house and flipping through a copy of *High Times* magazine. Inside the back cover was a feature that appeared in each issue called the "Hemp 100," in which readers would send in words or phrases that the magazine would rank with funny little cartoons. As I read them all, I was drawn to one in particular: the words "Fattie Bumballattie." I thought, *What a great emcee name*. It had a formidable flow and rolled with ease off the tongue. It was also easily rhyme-able. Plus, it had a dual meaning: 1) I was fat, and 2) I enjoyed puffing big ol' fatties. From that exact moment on, I was to be known as Fattie Bumballattie, which, over time, people have shortened to Fattie B.

A few years into touring with the band, my weight and health were heading for a danger zone. I was in such bad shape that I'd unknowingly begun suffering from diabetes. At one point, my condition triggered one of the most painful and embarrassing moments of my life.

It was the first night back from a month-long tour, during the last few days of which and I'd been experiencing numbness in my left inner thigh. I remember having difficulty urinating. It felt like I had to pee five gallons yet could only muster a drop or two. I went to bed early that night, uncomfortable and agitated.

I remember waking up around 3 a.m. and feeling like I had to piss fire. I stood up and turned and as I did I knocked over a small lamp on my bedside table. Not with my leg or elbow — with my swollen left nut! It was around the size of a FIFA soccer ball. I tried to convince myself it was all a horrible nightmare, but it was *more* than real. I literally started sobbing like a toddler.

I knew I had to get to the emergency room, so I put on my baggiest sweatpants and made my way out to my car. I started to climb into the driver's seat and realized I needed to put the seat all the way back just to fit my swollen sack under the steering wheel. I began to freak out, imagining that it was just going to keep inflating until it burst into a thousand shredded skin scraps.

I arrived at the hospital and was hurried into a room. After numerous tests, the docs determined that I had a urinary tract infection that had settled in behind the testicle, causing it to be become engorged.

Penicillin and ice packs brought it back to (almost normal) size; however, my sack today is like a 90-year-old lady's breasts — a long, wrinkled, and sad victim to the power of gravity. It is a constant reminder of my testicle terror.

You'd think that this incident would make someone deal with the severity of his own poor health, right?

Unfortunately, it took something even more serious than this to make me wake the fuck up.

NO PLACE LIKE 'NOME.

"Making your way in the world today
Takes everything you've got
Taking a break from all your worries
Sure would help a lot
Wouldn't you like to get away?

Sometimes you want to go
Where everybody knows your name
And they're always glad you came
you can see
Our troubles are all the same
You want to be where everyone
knows your name"

**Where Everybody Knows Your Name
(The Cheer's Theme)** by Gary Portnoy
Written by Gary Portnoy and Judy Hart Angelo
Released in 1982 on Argentum Records

I came of age professionally during Burlington's amazing live-band boom in the '90s. Beyond my own group, Belizbeha, there were many amazing live acts that enjoyed not only regional but national success. Phish, for example, signed their first major label deal with Elektra in 1991. The sheer number of great local acts made it nearly impossible to venture downtown on any given night and not catch a live band playing *somewhere*.

As the '90s came to an end, however, the recession hit and the music scene started to shift. Local club owners, realizing the value and growing popularity of DJs, began to focus their bookings accordingly. As a business decision, it was a no-brainer: Book a band (and an opening act) for $700-$1,000 and hope for a good turnout to recoup, or hire a DJ to play a certain format for $200-$300 and sell out regularly? The writing was, much too clearly, on the wall. Slowly, (whether for good or bad), DJs began to *take* these gigs from the bands.

One of the best examples of this transformation is the night I have helmed, Retronome. Created in 1996-'97 by (then club owner) Anne Rothwell and DJ Craig Mitchell, Retronome was a night that played to the nostalgia of the drinking-age demographic at the time through '80s dance floor cheese.

> All the songs you knew and loved to sing along to.
> Every week. Same time. Same place.
> In the bar where everybody knows your name.

Genius.

To get to Club Metronome — or the "'Nome," as it's called — you climb a flight of stairs out of the lobby of Nectar's, the legendary live music venue that gave birth to the band Phish in December of 1984. Their album *Picture Of Nectar* is named after the bar's original owner: Nectar Rorris.

Club Metronome has always kind of been Nectar's ugly step-sister, but a city the size of Burlington yearns for a true *dance* club — and not just hippie noodle dancing. Here in our obscure corner of the galaxy the 'Nome has satisfied the locals yearning to be self-proclaimed superstars for nearly 30 years.

In 1999, when my touring with Belizbeha began winding down, I took over for Craig Mitchell as the resident DJ of this popular night. I loved that I now had a job two blocks from my apartment that, once a week, for five hours, paid my bills and allowed me to *drink while I worked*. Who wouldn't want this perk, right? And then, as one month turned into two, and one year slipped into three, I began to realize certain facts about DJing a weekly formatted party (and they weren't all as good as free drinks):

1. The mathematics of song lengths never lie. As a DJ, we play most songs for about 2 to 2.5 minutes. 9 p.m. to 2 a.m. is five hours. Five hours equals 300 minutes. At 2.5 minutes a song, that's around 150-200 songs a week. Now just think about the '80s. Can you name 200 songs that are suitable for the dance floor? The list is thin, at best.

2. Fact #1 means that, no matter how you change up the order, you are basically playing the same 200-300 songs *every single week*. While many returning patrons loved this and looked forward to hearing "their song," as a DJ, it was the definition of maddening: doing the same thing over and over and expecting a different result.

3. I soon realized that I had to be that DJ that spent a lot of my time digging for alternate and remixed versions of songs. I wanted to keep my limited track listing as fresh as possible. And as mash-ups became popular, these helped break up the monotony as well.

4. The last thing I realized was that the people of the area absolutely loved this night. Whether screaming out the lyrics to "Don't Stop Believing" by Journey or dirty dancing to "Pour Some Sugar On Me" by Def Leppard, the good citizens of our region have used the familiarity of this era's songs to escape their weekly drama.

They have routinely left their trials and tribulations at the door and allowed the music to set them free.

A typical '80s night is a study in generational de-evolution. When we open the doors at 9 p.m., the first hundred or so patrons who make their way into the room are 35- to 50-ish and have already been sipping drinks for an hour or two. Roughly 70 percent of this group will be home by midnight, but they try to get their money's worth before making their exit.

The young adult demo is the next wave to fill the bar. This 25 to 30ish age group is just starting their evening of consumption, and many will be there close to last call a little before 2 a.m.

The third and last wave of customers to bum-rush the club are the 21- to 25-year-olds. They have been pre-gaming for a while, and I'd estimate that close to 80 percent of them are there to pound drinks and try to get laid.

Not that there's anything wrong with that.

As these three subdivisions overlap, the line out the door and down the block is often insane.

And the fact that people will wait a half-hour to 45 minutes in the rain or snow to get into a bar to hear '80s songs always blows me away. But, believe me, I'm glad they do.

As a method of helping some of my friends avoid the line and get in to see me, I've devised a method that is effective, efficient, and all the while entertaining to *me*.

When I first arrive to DJ, I use the website Urban Dictionary (www.urbandictionary.com) to search out a password. I like to find funny words that sound innocent but in actuality are dirty. Then I text them to my friends, who must whisper the words into the ear of the door girl (while both are completely unaware of their true meanings).

Like "Baby Toe." Sounds innocent enough, right? But according to Urban Dictionary, the term Baby Toe is "an unusually large clitorus." Or "Gobble Salad," which is "when Grandpa's balls are massaged by Grandma's turkey neck while receiving head." These are two of the more *reserved* choices.

Funny.

And gross.

Another funny (or sad) fact: I have officially been spinning at Club Metronome for so many years that I am now actually Djing for (and sharing drinks with) my friends' kids!

I'm simply doing all I can to reduce the generational gap.

"Go on and go free
Maybe you're too close to see
I can feel your body move
Does it mean that much to me
I can't go on singing the same theme
Cause can't you see
We've got everything
Baby
Even though you know...
Ev'ry time you go away,
You take a piece of me with you"

Every Time You Go Away by Paul Young
Written by Darryl Hall
Released in 1985 on Columbia

I am old enough to remember the magical powers and incomparability of a mixtape. An actual cassette tape, with a hand-picked and emotionally connected group of songs recorded for someone specific. Someone *special*. A hand-written label and a cover made of pictures cut out of magazines (usually magazines from my grandmother's bathroom) with dull scissors and pasted in just the right place with Elmer's Glue. Rough around the edges but smooth in its communications.

A *piece of me* created to be taken with *you*.

Back in the day, a mixtape was an incredible method of sharing all of the emotions, hopes, dreams, and fears from your heart and soul with another human being through the power of music. Put together 45 minutes on side A, 45 minutes on side B, and you had "hand-written" a love letter without touching pen, pencil, or paper. If you have ever received a mixtape from me, please know that you are on a short list of important people in my life. I've left a little bit of my innermost self on every single mix I've made for someone. That being said, it didn't take long for me to realize that the list of people worthy of that much effort, openness, and love was extremely small.

As technology has advanced, mixtapes have become CD mixtapes and now MP3 mixtapes. Throughout these format changes, I have stayed true to the original form in a few different ways. One: Although the mixes are now one long file, I like to treat them as two separate halves. So when I make a mix, I envision the first half as the introduction to both the music and the deeper message. The second half of my mix is always the reinforcement, the uniting of the two (music and message) and the conclusion. Two: I still like to make the covers, although now it is with Photoshop rather than scissors and glue. The cover is almost as important as the musical choices in clearly conveying the truth of your message. A good cover needs no explanation. A bad cover equals a bad mix. And Three: I always refer to it as a mixtape. One word. No spaces. No hyphens. It really doesn't matter if it's on a cassette, CD, MP3, DVD, or 4-track. To me, it is always called a *mixtape*.

That being said, in my humble opinion, there are certain rules that one should follow when making a true-to-form mixtape.

Let's discuss:

- Know the person.

It is important to understand (somewhat) just *whom* you are making the mix for. A small amount of knowledge of their musical tastes and personality are crucial. Not knowing either of these can shoot down your rocket ship.

- Be clear with your message.

The difference between an *"I'm in love with you"* mix and an *"I like soul music too"* mix is a very thin line.

- Name your mixtape.

Always. This goes hand-in-hand with the previous rule. Clear message = clear name = you're in the clear.

- Diversify.

Most definitely use a handful of songs that you know the recipient likes and that are directly connected to your message. However, it is your job to expand their musical library by thinking outside the box while continuing to express your proclamation.

No one wants to hear the same exact type of music for 90 minutes. On the flip side, though, too much randomness can equal loss of focus. Find the right combo and you win.

- Respect the power.

With great power comes great responsibility. Clearly. So do just that — be clear. Don't mislead. And, most of all, mean what you mix, damn it!

Last year, during an '80s night, I had a mixtape moment. And it includes one of the sad little regrets of my life.

For the last five years, exactly 15 minutes after the doors have opened every Saturday night, I've watched the same scene unfold in front of my eyes. A short, overweight, fortysomething gentleman shuffles into the club. He removes his coat, pours himself a glass of water from the cooler, and slowly sways his way into the center of the dance floor. The club having just opened, the patrons are few and far between. As more enter and the club slowly fills, our stubby little loner bobs by himself under the lasers and patiently waits for a song that makes him want to dance. This routine has been the same every single week. Through the passage of time, I have learned which songs make him want to shake his bon-bon and which ones earn me a look of disgust from afar. He's a man of few words.

In fact, I don't even know his real name. However, due to his physical resemblance to a certain cartoon bear, I've come to simply know him as "Paddington."

Last year, on a cold winter's night, I noticed Paddington was standing much closer to my booth than usual (he mostly stayed near the center of the dance floor). He looked more serious than normal, like he had something on his mind. Four to five songs later, I turned to find him standing directly next to me. He stared up at me in anticipation, a feeling I shared as I leaned in to excitedly hear his first-ever request: "Can I play a song for you?" I asked. He stuttered slightly, then mumbled to me, "I made this for you to play tonight." He then reached into the breast pocket of his corduroy suit jacket and slowly slid it out. A Memorex 90-minute cassette with "MIX 4 80's NITE" written on it with a silver Sharpie by what looked to be a six-year-old trying to learn cursive. I instinctively laughed a little out loud and said, "Oh, my man – I unfortunately don't have a cassette player here, so I can't play this. I'm sorry." He looked at me like I had just told him his cat was run over by a pickup. "I worked on it all day," he lamented.

"Yeah, I'm real sorry..." is all I had to offer back. He reluctantly took it back and slowly meandered off.

Amazed by his efforts, I told my wife all about it the next day.

She too found the interaction to be a mixture of suspended animation and sadness, but it was what she asked me next that really got me.

"What songs were on it?"

"Shit, I wish I knew. I didn't keep it. He took it back."

"Man, you're a dumbass."

She was right. I'll unfortunately never know what *magic* he had chosen as his own musical representation.

What I wouldn't give to have kept it so I could have listened to the entirety of its heartfelt glory.

RESPECT DUE.

"Tell the DJ to play your favorite tune,
then you know it's okay
What you found is happiness, now

Let this groove, get you to move, alright
Let this groove set in your shoes
Stand up, alright

We can boogie on down, down, down, down
Let's groove tonight
Share the spice of life
Baby slice it right
We're gonna groove tonight"

Let's Groove Tonight by Earth, Wind & Fire
Written by Maurice White, Wayne Vaughn
Released in 1981 on Columbia

Beyond the previously mentioned Tod Warner, there are a number of DJs who have inspired me, both stylistically and techincally, to play music the way I do today. Allow me to take a moment here to send gratitude and love out to them for being the spice of my music life:

1. DJ Jazzy Jeff
   Philadelphia
   He taught me early on (through his style and flavor) that hip-hop can be melodic *and* soulful.

2. DJ Z-Trip
   Phoenix
   Probably the biggest influence on my style. I have fully adopted his musical philosophy that you can play any style, any time, and make it all fit. Hip-hop, rock, funk, soul, rock or disco. One of the best ever. And my love for him only grew when I was lucky enough to spit rhymes with him live.

3. DJ Vinroc
   Queens
   His *So Much Soul* mix series are among my all-time favorites. Like melted butter on the blends.

4. Questlove
    Philadelphia
   Known much more as the drummer for the hip-hop crew The Roots, Questlove is also a DJ. I've seen him multiple times and have the ultimate respect for him as a musical educator. He plays the hits that the kids want to hear, but much of his set is dedicated to teaching — making you learn by listening to something you maybe had never heard before.

5. Mark Farina
    Chicago
   A true master of the art of mixing beats, he would easily have three or four different songs playing at once. His *Mushroom Jazz* series are also at the top of my all-time favorites lists of mixes.

6. DJ Luis Calderin
    Miami/Burlington
   My good friend Luis definitely had a huge impact on my early hip-hop education. His radio show "40 Ounces of Funky Flavors" on the UVM station WRUV 90.1 FM was my favorite (along with Melo Grant's "Cultural Bunker" show). From the early to mid-'90s, he educated me to what music was hot and, later on, as my friend, showed me what being cool was really all about. One of my most reliable (and best) friends to this day.

7. DJ A-Dog (aka Andy Williams)
    St. Albans/Burlington
   A-Dog was hands down the greatest DJ to ever come out of the state of Vermont and, amazingly, an even better human being. Andy and I were friends and bandmates for almost 20 years. Sadly, we all lost him in 2013 to complications from leukemia, but his music and memory live on. He embodied tasteful music selections, elite scratching, and originality in every mix he produced — all in one stylistic package. A true artist and a world-class talent, he was someone we were all lucky enough to call our own here in Burlington. The best part about Andy was, as good as he was as a Dj, he was an even person. Rest in power, Dog. I love you and miss you every day.

8. DJ Craig Mitchell
    Saginaw/Burlington
   Probably the biggest influence on me both personally and as a jockey. His mantra that "Life = Music" resonates with my passion and love for this craft. The multiple times he and I have shared the decks are among the best times of my blessed days on this earth. And as a friend of 25 years, he is someone who has inspired me to be better in all facets of living my life to the fullest. I strive to be worthy of his respect, friendship, and love and have nothing but the utmost admiration for him. Craigerz!

Beyond being good friends with Craig, Andy, and Luis, I am blessed to have had the opportunity to meet each of these other DJs. I didn't bore them with my man-crush details or bother them while they worked. I personally think that would be rude. Rather, I just chose to simply sit off to the side, observe, and try to learn from them.

But as a DJ on a much smaller level, as well as one who helms a weekly themed night, I expect to be approached and to have to deal with the one word all DJs dread most:

REQUESTS!

A BRIBE CALLED REQUEST.

"And imagine (just imagine) the sound
Let the music (let the music)
Put you in a zone
I get lost, lost inside a groove
When you do the things you do

Hey! Mr. DJ, play that song for me
Hey! Mr. DJ, jam all night long
Hey! Mr. DJ, play that song for me
Keep it coming Mr. DJ"

Hey DJ by World Famous Supreme Team
Written by Larry Price, Malcolm McLaren, Ronald Larkins Jr. and Stephen Hague
Released in 1984 on Island

Although completely unbeknownst to most, there is a certain etiquette inherent to politely and properly requesting a song.

For the unaware, these rules include:

- Avoid making a request while we are mixing or speaking with someone else.
- Try to request a song that fits into the night's format.
- Try not to request a song that is playing *as you request it*.
- Try to not request a different song by the same artist that is playing while you request it.
- Say please and thank you.
- Don't be fucking rude.

I design my nights around songs' beats per minutes (BPM). So, if I'm playing a tune at 120-130 BPMs, it might just take me a few songs to get to your request for George Michael's "Freedom" (which is around 90 BPM). But please — *please* — be patient. I promise ... I will get there.

I have discovered that the best response to *all* requests is a big smile, a head nod, and a "Sure thing, no problem." Even if I have no intention of ever getting to it, this quells the anger that would most certainly follow if I said what I was really thinking: "Hell to the mother-fucking no."

And FYI, your sad face does not make the DJ sorry for you and want to play your request.

I want to be absolutely clear here:

I love 95 percent of the people who approach me with kindness and praise, but there are the 5 percent who don't think before they speak.

For this special group (and the sheer entertainment value for my fellow small-time DJs worldwide), I present the following list:

HOW YOU CAN ANNOY A DJ

- Ask us if we takes requests then have no clue what you want to hear.

- Ask for a song that nobody will dance to (including you).

- Complain that no one else likes the song that's playing (when the dance floor is completely full).

- Make silly "scratching" poses at us like you are a DJ too.

- Fight with us about what year a song was released.

- Get all of your friends to ask for the same song that we already refused to play for you.

- Grab or touch our equipment while we're playing.

- Get so drunk that you think the DJ booth is the bar or the coat check.

- Ask for the same song *every single time* you are in the club.

- Wear so much cologne or perfume that it makes our eyes water.

- Think your $2 tip will get your song on next.

- Ask for a song and then stand by our booth until we play it.

- Ask us to go online and download your requests (that we don't have or simply don't want to play).

- Keep demanding a shout out. All. Night. Long.

- Tell us the other DJ always plays your song — when there is no other DJ.

- Ask us to hand out flyers or announce a show from a rival dance club.

- Keep asking for requests after we are closed.

- Lay a big stinky fart right next to the DJ booth.

- And, lastly, but by no means least, inform us that you are rolling deep with a bachelorette party.

An actual song request list from an '80s night.

NIGHT FEVER - Bee Gees
ROCK THE CASBAH - CLASH
STAND BY ME - CLASH
JUST LIKE A DREAM - CURE
LADIES NIGHT - KOOL + GANG
FLASHDANCE
VIDEO KILLED RADIO STAR
WORD UP - CAMEO
DANCING IN THE MOONLIGHT
THIS OLD HEART OF MINE - Isley Brothers
BADLANDS - Springsteen
BREATHE - TALKING HEADS
SUPER FREAK - RICK JAMES
THE LOVE I LOST - HAROLD MELVIN

LADIES FIRST?

"On disco lights, your name will be seen
You can fulfill all your dreams
Party here, party there, everywhere
This is your night, baby, you've got to be there

Oh yes it's ladies night
and the feeling's right
Oh yes it's ladies night,
Oh what a night, oh what a night"

Ladies Night by Kool & The Gang
Written by George M. Brown and Kool & The Gang
Released in 1980 on DeLite

A bachelorette party is the last chance for the bride-to-be to go out with her closest friends and celebrate her upcoming married life.

While it's supposed to be a bonding experience filled with laughter, tears, and talk of both the past and the future, there are women that (sadly) use their bachelorette party as an excuse to act like low-class trash.

It's not that *all* bachelorette parties are annoying. But, in my decade and a half of experience in dealing with them, I would guesstimate the percentage that are annoying to be at around 60 percent. From the silly games to the penis straws and the annoying requests, most DJs dread seeing a bachelorette party headed their way. Add to these the fact that most of these ladies hardly ever regularly drink or go out, but during these parties consume alcohol like they are 22 again, and it is a no-fail formula for a DJ migraine.

Here is the best piece of advice I can share with a Maid of Honor: It's all in how you approach us. If you come at me in a humble and friendly manner and ask for songs for the bride when I can fit them in, I've got you covered. However, bum-rush my booth with either a long list of songs that you annoy me to play or demand that I announce the bride's name three to four times per hour? Well, my dear, we aren't going to be best buddies. And add in some dumb-ass bride scavenger hunt you scream at me to announce ("Not now, but right fucking now!")? Well, you can pretty much guarantee that I'm farting in your face in my mind.

Teachable moment here, kiddos.

"You catch more flies with honey
than you ever will with vinegar."

That goes for everything in life.

Be nice = (maybe) you get your way.
Be mean = you definitely fucking lose.

Every time.

I really don't mind giving a friendly bride a shout out in a packed club to make her feel like her night is *special*. But, once we do that for one, seven other girls immediately run to the booth with names for us to shout out as well. Birthdays. Anniversaries. Other brides. Then they get all agro at me for spreading the announcements out so they are one at a time. Don't you ladies understand that I am attempting to give each of you your *own* individual spotlight moment?

Grrrrrr....

And then there are the condom balloons and inflatable four-foot dicks the bridesmaids carry around. Or the edible candy cock necklaces they ask *me* to eat. WTF? Since when did phallic symbols equal the end of single life? I thought you were giving up all of the other penises you'd slutted your way through to get to the keeper.

All of this deep-seeded aggravation stems from the weeks that have turned into years that have turned into decades of the same parties, different brides.

But one particular bride not only gave me high blood pressure (and some of her DNA), but also cost me money.

This was probably around 2008, when I was still DJ'ing from my little cave-booth behind the stage. A bachelorette party of seven arrived about 10 minutes after we had opened our doors. They had been pre-gaming, so they were already slurring and full of good old-fashioned sexual tension-filled energy. The bride rushed my window and announced, as loudly as she could, that this was now "her night" and tossed a crumpled up napkin at me filled with requests. I smiled, took a deep breath, and congratulated her. I informed her that I would get to them all, but it was early and many of them were popular requests, so some of them would be played a little later when the club would be full.

She scrunched up her nose in angst, turned, and stomped back to her brat pack. I began playing some of her songs and honestly felt like I had done her right by working through about half of the lengthy list by 10:30.

Well, she didn't agree. Or care. Or have breath that smelled very good. She returned to protest. Only now half of her chunky little body was jammed into my window and she was berating me (and my skills as a jockey). I again took a second to breathe (a technique all DJs know and use often — as opposed to back-handing a bitch) and politely reminded her that I had already played nearly half of her songs. I also reminded her that she hadn't even said "thank you" yet.

That comment (and the six kamikaze shots I'd watched her knock back) sent her over the edge. She reached in and snatched back her napkin list. She screamed out the names of the songs that I had yet to play and demanded that they be put on next. She boldly educated me on the fact that she was "very good friends" with the owner. When I asked that person's name, she slurred the name of a former bartender who was fired four months prior. Realizing I had no chance to win this battle, I patronizingly murmured, "No problem. Thanks for your help."

That little *"thanks for your help"* line was the straw that broke this thirsty camel's back. She glared at me, enraged that I was uninterested in her demands. I assumed that if I just ignored her (and her halitosis), she would eventually wander off and bitch about me to her posse. I slid my headphones back on so I couldn't hear her and began to mix in the next song. That's when she did it.

She reached her arm in and extended it as far as she could. As I looked up, what happened next seemed to proceed in super slow motion. She turned her wrist and began pouring her pint glass of gin and tonic upside down, emptying the entire contents directly into my mixer. As I froze in complete amazement, she then hocked up a huge loogie and proceeded to spit it directly in the center of my Tribe Called Quest T-shirt. As it slowly ran down my torso, I turned towards the amps and watched as the volume meters began to fade until all anyone in the club could hear was static, buzzing, and then... total silence. The mixer was completely fried and I had a giant snotty phlegm ball on my gut.

I had her tossed out by security and was forced to play a pre-recorded mix for the remainder of the night. The mixer was less than a month old and was 100 percent destroyed. She agreed to pay for it but never returned any of the subsequent messages we left for her.

The only thing that makes me able to even tell this story without wanting to shank someone is that, soon afterwards, her fiancé cheated on her with one of her bridesmaids and they never got married.

He must have wanted a lady who wasn't a spitter.

UNCOMFORTABLY NUMB.

"Hello,
Is there anybody in there?
Just nod if you can hear me
Is there anyone at home?

Come on now
I hear you're feeling down
Well, I can ease your pain
And get you on your feet again

There is no pain, you are receding
A distant ship, smoke on the horizon
You are only coming through in waves
Your lips move
but I can't hear what you're saying

I have become comfortably numb"

Comfortably Numb by Pink Floyd
Written by David Gilmour & Roger Waters
Released in 1980 on Columbia

In the early 2000s, I started DJing a few nights a week at a new club in town aimed at the adult business demographic. It featured delicious food and a fancy interior and sold higher-priced drinks (mostly in an attempt to eliminate the riff-raff). However, for some unexplained reason, the owners made the ill-advised decision (intentionally or not) to make the venue's name the same as the slang term for the "morning-after pill."

That's right. It was called Plan B.

Anyhoo, during the winter months I did a weekly gig on Wednesdays. As most club owners know, Wednesdays are generally the toughest night (numbers wise). During the brutal Vermont winters, Wednesdays are even slower. One very quiet, cold, and snowy February evening, I was spinning to a nearly empty room. Noticing there was just a single table with three ladies (plus the two staff members working bar), Plan B's manager told me to just end early and come have a drink with them. Happy to do so, I closed up my equipment and sidled up to the bar. As I awaited my martini, I looked over at the trio of ladies at the table to my immediate right and realized that one of them was trouble waiting to happen. For the purpose of this story, I will call her Luna (mainly because she was a completely unhinged *lunatic*).

You see, earlier that year, during a rough night of drinking, I had hooked up with her at a friend's house. We came as close to sex as you can come without achieving full penetration (i.e. just the tip), but something about her told me to back it up, pack it up, and hit the road, Jack. I can't even remember what reason I gave, but I was up and out of there quicker than a getaway car.

Back to that night at Plan B: Luna was grilling me from her seat at the table, and, the more I glanced up, the more I noticed the intensity of her gape.

I knew one of the other girls sitting with her, so I made the ill-fated decision to walk over to say hello and (hopefully) cut drama off at the pass. I smiled and pulled up a chair and started some small talk. The other two ladies were friendly, but Luna was stern and, quite honestly, scaring me more than a little. I got flustered, so I stood up and announced I was going to the rest room. The other two females with Luna thought that idea sounded great as well and stood up to walk that way with me. I left my barely touched martini on the table alone with Luna. During our walk across the club, I asked the other two if I had any reason to be nervous or frightened of her. They laughed and reassured me that she was "harmless" and that I should really give her a second chance.

After I came back from the restroom, Luna was sitting alone. I asked where the others had gone and she replied that they were out smoking a cigarette. About 30 seconds of awkward silence and two gulps of my drink later, I stood and excused myself to step out for some air where (hopefully) I would find the other girls.

I remember stepping out onto the deck and noticing how beautiful the falling snow looked. It was coming down at a pretty good rate, with big, fluffy flakes settling softly all around me. The streets were completely quiet, and I just stared up at the sky while the flakes peacefully fell. I began to feel a little light-headed and somewhat strange. I was trying, with some inexplicable trouble, to get a grip on reality. And, then, I literally just blacked out.

What happened next was the absolute weirdest night of my life.

When I came to, I was walking in a snowstorm. It was a full-on blizzard and I was cold and alone, trudging along the side on the road. I knew I was *walking*, but had no idea where I was, where I was walking to, or how I had come to be there at all. When I finally started to regain focus and get a grasp of where I was (which took about five more minutes of walking to achieve), I slowly realized that I was about 10 miles out of town and headed south on Route 7.

I had wandered away from the club and walked all the way out of town. Still walking and still headed south, I had to literally say to myself out loud, "Hey, asshole! Stop moving! You're going the wrong direction!"

So I stopped dead in my tracks. I turned back north and began retracing my steps, realizing fully now that I was tripping my balls off in a full-on whiteout. I was anxious and alone and had somehow lost my cell phone.
Then it hit me: Luna had roofied me! I had only consumed about half of that martini, and I knew now why the look in her eyes had terrified me to my core.

There was no traffic in either direction. I didn't know for sure, but with how far I had walked, it had to be close to 4 a.m.. At the pace I was walking and shivering, I wouldn't get home until at least 5:30 a.m. or 6 a.m.. Then I saw it: two dim car headlights slowly approaching in the distance from behind me and headed north. As the car got closer, I literally walked in the middle of the road and flagged it down. It was a cab! I was saved!

The cabbie pulled up to me and rolled down his window. I begged him for a ride but was informed that it was almost 7:00 a.m. and that, with the almost foot of snow from the storm, he had a backup of at least five calls waiting for rides to work. Desperate, I blurted out a last-ditch offer:

"I'm tripping my balls off and I'm scared. I'll give you $100 cash to take me to my apartment on Church Street." He paused, groaned, and then barked, "Jesus Christ. Get in."

I made it home and paid him. I sat up tripping for another four hours, trying to thaw my now frozen and uncomfortably numb feet and brain.

I never saw Luna again but heard through the grapevine that she had drugged another guy about a year earlier. Thank the good Lord I had escaped her wrath.

I promised myself at that exact moment that my days of hooking up with strange females were 100 percent finished.

At least until the next one....

THE PRICE YOU PAY.

"An angel's smile is what you sell
You promise me heaven then put me through hell
Chains of love got a hold on me
When passion's a prison you can't break free

Shot through the heart and you're to blame
Darlin' you give love a bad name"

You Give Love A Bad Name by Bon Jovi
Written by Jon Bon Jovi, Richie Sambora & Desmond Child
Released in 1986 by Mercury

When you make the decision to be a DJ, there are many perks that make your life sweeter, including the amazing pay, free passes to shows, increased popularity, the ability to drink on the job, and the rewarding feelings you receive from helping people to have some much-needed fun.

I personally have reaped many amazing rewards from this profession (that I will discuss further in an upcoming chapter).

However, the other side of the coin is that there are repercussions to this career choice that can slowly *ruin* both you (and your life partner).

Let's discuss the negative side-effects this job has on you (the DJ) and, subsequently, why your wife/girlfriend/boyfriend wants to kill you because of them:

WHY CHOOSING TO BE A DJ IS DETRIMENTAL

1. As DJs, we can never go to a club and just have fun anymore. This is mainly because once you mix music for a living, you hear things differently. I can't just go out and enjoy myself like I did before. Now, I find myself analyzing the DJ's skills and song choices. If I hear a song I play, I mock his choice of follow-up tune in my mind if it's not one I would use. If I even try to talk to my wife about this one, she looks at me like I'm an asshole.

2. I critique his mixes way too harshly, mainly because (in my mind) I feel like I could do better. And please don't let him play a song way faster or slower than it's normal BPM. This is like fingernails on a chalkboard to DJs. We *cannot* ignore it and have to acknowledge it. Or if he trainwrecks a mix? Oh, man.... I know better than to even say anything about these out loud to my wife (unless she brings them up first, in which case I get excited to bash him with her). I'm a bad, bad person.

3. Everytime I hear a song, (whether in a club, the car, a store or at home) I have to remember the song title and artist or I lose my shit. Add to that my obsession with finding the orignal sample used in the tune. God forbid I can't remember any one of these while my wife is talking to me because, as I frantically Google the answers and stop listening to her, I'm properly and rightfully scolded. I can't imagine how annoying this is for her. Sorry, baby. It's an addiction. A true sickness.

4. Another addiction: Guessing song BPMs. As a DJ, we use these tempos to blend songs, so reckognizing one simply by listening is paramount. So I play the annoying game of guessing the tempo out loud, then using the BPM counter on my cell

phone to tap out the song's count and see if I am right. If I am , I feel like a champ. If I'm off, I feel like a failure at life. Either way, my wife is driven to drink.

5. The biggest sickness (and the one that may need an intervention): downloading and collecting music. This drives my wife crazy on many levels. As she tries in vain to peacefully watch her DVR'ed episode of *Dateline*, I continually play snippets of downloaded remixes and annoy the shit out of her. There are nights where I'll find a blog that's ripe with free downloads and spend six to seven hours on it. My wife, to put it kindly, is not impressed with my use of our time together here.

6. What I call the In-Sync Syndrome. I'm constantly noticing when things inadvertantly sync up to music tempos. A TV with the sound off and some music playing, a car's windshield wiper in the car with the radio on, even the tempo of a person's walk while out with headphones on. Everytime I notice one of these occurences I give myself an imaginary high-five. WTF is wrong with me?

7. When my wife and I are out and I hear a remix of a song I've never heard before — big trouble.

Whatever conversation she and I are having is immedietly over in my brain, and all of my attention is focused on hearing the remix and trying to find out who made it and when.

8. Loss of valuable time. I *never* have a weekend off. Friday and Saturday nights are the prime DJ nights, so forget any normal weekend activities (like friends' holiday parties, watching big playoff/tournament games, and even just going away for the weekend with your significant other).

9. Groupies and/or flirting. It's part of your job and can be annoying to you (since you often have to pretend to like or be nice to those you might not), but imagine how shitty it is for your partner to sit by and watch this all go down.

10. Your Facebook page is hijacked. As much as you try to resist, your page becomes a constant ad for your gigs and all of the songs and other DJs you are obsessed with. I can't even imagine how annoying this for my friends who don't give a rip about me as a DJ and just know me as Kyle. Sorry, everyone. Here's a cat video...

11. Lastly, hearing loss.

    Not only are you in a club setting multiple nights a week (which is detrimental enough to your hearing), but you constantly have headphones on blast wrapped around your ears. My hearing is bad enough now that I miss parts of conversations and have to have the TV so loud that it annoys those around me. And I'm only in my 40s.

    I see a hearing aid in my future. And an angry wife.

All this and more can be yours thanks to playing music for a living.

Did I say I love being a DJ?

Because, believe it or not, I really do.

LE FREAK. I SHREIKED.

"Now when freaks get dressed to go out at night
They like to wear leather jackets, chains and spikes
They wear rips and zippers all in their shirts
Real tight pants and fresh mini skirts
All kinds of colors runnin' through their hair
And you could just about find a freak anywhere
But then again, you could know someone all their life
But might not know they're a freak unless you see them at night, 'cause

The freaks come out at night!"

The Freaks Come Out At Night by Whodini
Written by Jalil Hutchins
Released in 1984 on Jive/Arista

Around six years ago, we renovated Club Metronome and moved my DJ booth from out behind the stage to an elevated open stand out front facing the stage. There were pluses and minuses to this. Plus #1: I could now see the entire club from my 8-foot perch and, therefore, could read the mood of the room much more easily. Plus #2: I was now about 4 feet from the bar (making drink access more efficient). Major minus: I couldn't sneak a girl in the back for a handjob.

Anyway, from this viewpoint, I witnessed a smorgasbord of reality TV, including attempted hook-ups, failed hook-ups, and bad idea hook-ups. But what I witnessed on one particular night will never be erased from my memory banks.

I noticed a tall, shapely woman standing at the bar. She stood about 6 feet 2 inches (with 4-inch heels) and was quite attractive. She had long, dark brown hair, and her exotic features were similar to Eva Mendes. She wore leggings and a tuxedo shirt, topped off by a gold bowtie. She approached my booth and, with a southern accent, politely requested a song. She was so nice (and sexy) that I agreed to play it right away. After I did, she again came back over, thanked me, and wondered if I might be able to fit one more in. As I chatted with her, she told me that she was visiting from Texas and that it was her birthday.

I asked her if she wanted a birthday shot. She nodded, and we scooted over to the bar where we shared one. As I hopped back up into my booth, I slid her one of my mix CDs and wished her a happy birthday. She smiled and skipped out to dance as I played her second request.

Soon thereafter, I noticed her standing at the corner of the bar, head down in folded arms and looking just a little bit ill (like she might need to hurl). I wondered if my gesture of a birthday shot had sent her over the edge and scanned the room, looking for a member of the club's security to give her some assistance (and maybe get her a glass of water). Not immediately seeing anyone that worked there, I returned my attention to my mixer and prepped to blend in the next song.

At the exact moment I changed tunes, I heard the cry from a female patron standing next to her at the bar. "She's pissing!" the girl shrieked, pointing at the birthday girl. I turned to look, but her back was turned to me, and all I could see was a three-inch stream of steaming hot pee shooting down between her legs. Then, amazingly, it actually got *worse*.

A male patron on the other side pointed directly at her crotch and yelled (even louder than the girl had), "She's got a cock!"

That's when the *southern belle* turned and allowed me to see her sausage swinging and shooting piss all over the bar and a few drunks' shoes.

Security quickly came and escorted her out and returned to mop up the river she (or he) had left behind. I remember the discussion among the people who had witnessed it, and their perspectives were all pretty much the same as mine: that none of us had any idea whatsoever that the Eva look-alike was *not* a woman.

But one thing not surprising about it at all?

The simple fact that it occurred here, in Burlington and at Club Metronome:

        Proud refuge to all freaks and geeks.

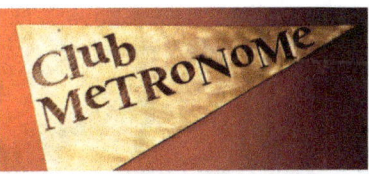
The sign leading up the stairs to the club.

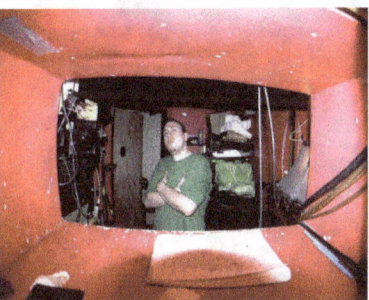
The view from the stage into my old booth.

Another shot peeking into my booth.

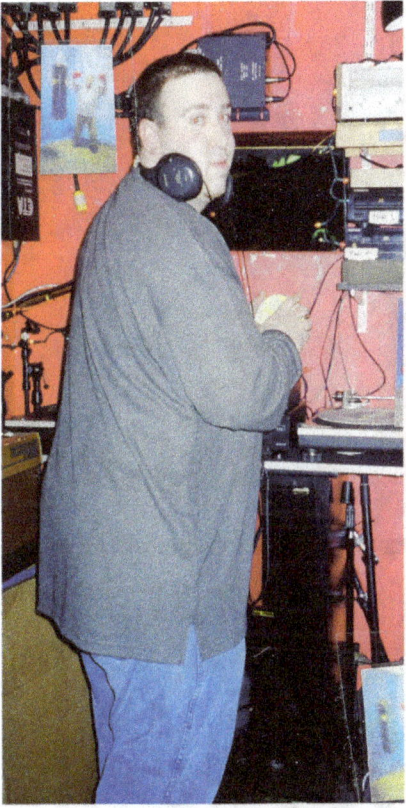
Me inside my old DJ booth at Club Metronome.

The originator of 80's night, Craig Mitchell, in the early days.

FLYERS.

With some of my idols.

Meeting the legend, DJ Z-Trip.

DJ Questlove and I after his set.

With DJ Luis Calderin.

DJ Craig Mitchell and I.

With the late, great DJ A-Dog.

The renovated Club Metronome.

The view from the newer, elevated DJ booth. The renovated bar.

The lounge area (with my artwork on the walls).

The dancefloor at Club Metronome.

Me, myself and I.

Press photo in front of my artwork.

At my heaviest weight (435 pounds).

Channel live.

Live on stage.

B-Scene cover July 2009

Champlain View cover Spring 2003

YOU DON'T SAY.

"*Say, say, say what you want,*
But don't play games with my affection,
Take, take, take what you need,
But don't leave me with no direction.

You, you, you can never say,
That I'm not the one who really loves you,
I pray, pray, pray every day,
That you'll see things, girl like I do."

Say Say Say by Paul McCartney
Written by Paul McCartney & Michael Jackson
Released in 1983 on Columbia

I truly love being a DJ.

I fully recognize just how blessed I am to be paid to do this for a living and that I get to play such an integral part in helping patrons have a good time and forget their daily stress and strife. I love making people smile, laugh, dance, and sing along.

But a teeny tiny part of me just wishes some folks, before approaching me, would take a second to pause and really think about what they were going to say (before they open up and let it come tumbling out).

That being said, I present...

ACTUAL SHIT
ACTUAL PEOPLE
ACTUALLY SAID TO ME:

- "Hey, are you like the DJ 'n' shit, bro?"

- "Play something with a beat." Or, "Play something dancey." Or, even better, "Play something good."

- Or, best of all: "Play anything *but this*."

- "How many more songs till you play *our* song?"

- "Can you do that wikki-wikki thing?"

- "Hey, I'm a DJ too. Can I spin?"

- "What kinda stuff do you play?" Or, "Which songs do you have?" Or, "Do you have a book of songs we can look at?"

- "Yo, you got an Ipod hook up? Play this off my phone, bro."

- "Not sure what it's called, but it's like dumm-dee-dee dat doopy-doop-doop. Yeah, play that one."

- "What song is next? What about after that one?"

- "Can you replay this song as an instrumental so I can karaoke on it?'

- "Is it cool if I just set my drink on your DJ table for, like, five minutes?"

- "Can you play it next? We're about to leave." Or, "Play my song next. This song sucks ass."

- "You already played that one? But I wasn't here yet." Or, "Can you just play it again? I was in the bathroom."

- "I took a poll of the crowd and we *all* want hear Garth Brooks now."

- "Do we have to listen to *this* music?" Or, "Is *this* all you're gonna play tonight?"

- "Change the beat up, yo. You're just playing the same song."

- And, lastly, one of my all-time favorites: "If you play my song, I'm definitely getting laid."

* THESE ARE A FEW OF THE AMAZING WAYS I'VE BEEN ASKED FOR SONGS *

These all begin with: "Can you please play...

- ...two chicks and a pair of dice?"

What they meant:
"Two Tickets to Paradise" by Eddie Money

- ...Alex the seal?"

What they meant:
"Our Lips Are Sealed" by The Go-Go's

- ...Shaving all my muff for you?"

What they meant:
"Saving All My Love For You" by Whitney Houston

- ...Son likes to bang cock?"

What they meant:
"One Night In Bangcock" by Murray Head

- ...Keep it common law?"

What they meant:
"Keep It Coming Love" by KC & The Sunshine Band

- ...Rock the cat box?"

What they meant:
"Rock the Casbah" by The Clash

- ...Might as well face it, you're a dick with a glove?"

What they meant:
"Addicted to Love" by Robert Palmer

- ...Totally blitzed by a fart?"

What they meant:
"Total Eclipse of the Heart" by Bonnie Tyler

- ...I got my first real sex dream?"

What they meant:
("Got my first real six string...") from "Summer of '69" by Bryan Adams

And my all-time personal favorite...

- ...Anus is the center hole?"

What they meant:
("Angel is a centerfold") from "Centerfold" by J. Geils Band

True story, bro.

AIN'T NO HALF STEPPIN'.

"I was a fiend, before I became a teen
I melted microphone
instead of cones of ice cream
Music orientated so when hip-hop was
originated
Fitted like pieces of puzzles, complicated
'Cause I grabbed the mic and try to say,
'Yes y'all!'
They tried to take it, and say that I'm too
small
Cool, 'cause I don't get upset
I kick a hole in the speaker, pull the plug,
then I jet"

Microphone Fiend by Eric B. & Rakim
Written by Eric Barrier & Rakim Allah
Released in 1988 on RCA

I don't want to sound like the grumpy old man who bemoans "Now Frank Sinatra — that's *real* music right there." But I pretty much am when I talk about how I truly feel about the state of modern hip-hop music: It's horrible.
Basically, in my humble opinion, there has been a whole lot of garbage released since the golden era ended (1984-1998).

Maybe I feel this way since I came of age during that period of fertility in rhyme, when there was a potpourri of styles and everyone was (imagine this) *unique*. Unlike today, where it seems everyone just tries to pump out carbon copies of whatever is the hot style of the moment, the '80s demanded individuality. Both the wordplay and musical techniques were dictated by an artist's geographic community and not simply by iTunes downloads.

I also loved how many of the beats from the '80s were old disco, soul, and funk samples — grooves that owed their debt to the good time block parties that rap was originally birthed from. In fact, many of these tracks hold up quite well over all these years, retaining their feel-good party vibes even today.

My heartbeat for early rap still pounds strongly, and I get the same emotions now when I play certain songs (while DJing) that I did the first time I heard them:

Joy. Happiness. Energy. Respect. Love.
What I call **"the vibes."**

When a song or beat gave you "the vibes," you couldn't help but smile and, even more so, couldn't wait to share it with your buddies. So, to counter-balance all the frustration certain silly comments and songs have slowly brought to my soul (and to this book), I present this:

My All-Time Top 10 favorite '80s Rap Songs:

10. "I Got It Made" by Special Ed
1989

One of my all-time favorite beats sampled from Ripple's "I Don't Know What It Is, But It Sure Is Funky."
Try to *not* nod your head to it.

9. "The Breaks" by Kurtis Blow
1980

While many believed this groove was sampled from The Doobie Brothers' "Long Train Running,"
it wasn't and is all original.

8. "Brass Monkey" by Beastie Boys
1987

Confession time: I stole Volkswagen emblems from the front of students' cars in the parking lot of UVM when I was in high school to wear on a chain like King Ad-Rock.

7. "Peter Piper" by Run-DMC
1986

The combo of nursery rhymes and the beat from Bob James' "Take Me To The Mardi Gras" makes this genius.

6. "The Show" by Doug E. Fresh & Slick Rick
1985

The *Inspector Gadget* theme song sample always takes me back to being a kid on Saturday mornings.

5. "Me, Myself & I" by De La Soul
1988

I loved their freedom of style and especially loved the sample from "(Not Just) Knee Deep" by Funkadelic.

4. "It Takes Two" by Rob Base & DJ E-Z Rock
1988

The greatest party rap song of all time, it perfectly samples "Think (About It)" by Lynn Collins.

3. "Ain't No Half Steppin" by Big Daddy Kane
1988

The "Blind Alley" by The Emotions sample is made for rhyming on. Period.

2. "Children's Story" by Slick Rick
1989

This song was sampled in Montell Jordan's "This Is How We Do It" in 1995. A 100 percent feel-good groove.

(and, drum roll please...)
1. "Paid In Full"
(Coldcut's "Seven Minutes of Madness" Remix)
by Eric B. & Rakim
1987

Coldcut's extended version made this one of the best rap singles of all-time (hands down).

YOU'RE KILLIN' ME SMALLS.

"I used to love her
But I had to kill her
I used to love her   Mm, yeah
But I had to kill her
I had to put her, ooh, six feet under
And I can still hear her complain

She bitched so much, she drove me nuts
And now I'm happier this way
Yeah Whoa Oh yeah"

Used To Love Her by Guns n' Roses
Written by Izzy Stradlin & Axl Rose
Released in 1988 on Geffen

Setting: State police barracks interrogation room.
Williston, Vermont. June 12, 2012.

1:35 p.m.

MKT = M.K. Thompson
SAF = FBI Special Agent Ken Forrester

Thompson is sitting on a chair at the table, handcuffed and with shackles around his ankles.

Special Agent Forrester enters room to begin the questioning. The agent sits directly across from the prisoner, slides a folder of papers and photos across the table at Thompson, and unveils a digital recording device. The agent then proceeds to begin recording.

SAF: Mr. Thompson, my name is Special Agent Forrester. I understand you would like to tell me about these murders and your role in them. Is that correct?

MKT: (Mumbles.)

SAF: Please speak loudly and clearly, sir.

MKT: Ummm, yes ... yes sir.
I guess I am ready to talk about them.
All of them.

SAF: *All of them?*
How many *songs* did you actually kill?

MKT: Five. But that's only because you caught me.
I would have kept going ... they were... mocking me.

SAF: Five?! Jesus Christ!
We only knew about two.
Let's just take these one at a time here, OK?

MKT: Yeah, OK.
Just so you know, though, I'm not a bad person.
I just have bad thoughts. And despise bad songs.

You see, it's just ... these songs...
they keep coming back. Every fucking week.
And I just couldn't take it anymore. I lost it.

SAF: OK, sir. Please just start from the beginning.

MKT: The first one was "Mony Mony" by Billy Idol. I had nothing but pure hatred for that song and everybody yelling about *"riding that fucking pony."* After having to play it every week for 14 straight years, it started to become painful. A tune turned tumor. I couldn't escape it. The voice in my brain told me the only way to make it stop was to kill it off.

SAF: The "voice in your brain"?
What does this voice sound like?

MKT: A lot like Estelle Getty from *Golden Girls* on sizzurp. She is 100 percent pure evil.

SAF: OK then ... that's not weird at all.
So, how exactly did you kill "Mony Mony"?

MKT: I dug a hole in the desert and buried that slut alive.

SAF: But that was just the start of your work, wasn't it?

MKT: Yes, sir. Once I realized how easy it was to pull off and how good it felt to eliminate it from my playlist, I kinda' went a little berserk.

SAF: What does that mean exactly?

MKT: It snowballed.
One led to two, which led to three and so on.

SAF: Let's just stay with one at a time, please sir.

MKT: OK. Next was "Girls Just Wanna Have Fun" by Cyndi Lauper. Man, that fucker was annoying as hell.
So I doused it with gasoline and set it on fire.
I happily watched it burn to the ground.

Then I took a nice long piss on its ashes.

SAF: You sick fuck. Oh Cyndi. Please continue.

MKT: Three and four were a KOGO — Kill One, Get One free. First was "Come On Eileen" by Dexy's Midnight Runners. Mr. Forrester, do you know what's better than cheese on crackers?

SAF: No. Please enlighten me.

MKT: Cum on Eileen.

SAF: Let's skip the bad DJ jokes, sir. Just tell me what happened to that song?

MKT: I hated that bitchy little bastard. I wanted it to suffer like I did when I had to play it. So I locked it in a room with 10,000 killer bees.

SAF: Oh, my lord. What was the second half?

MKT: I sent "Love Shack" by The B-52's a text that "Come On Eileen" was in trouble. When "Love Shack" showed up to help, I clubbed it over the head and tossed its body in a wood chipper. Suck on that, *tin roof.*

SAF: I'm going to be honest. I'm more than a litle bit scared of you. But that's only four. You said there were a total of five. What was the last song?

MKT: It was last weekend. Rick Springfield's "Jessie's Girl". A little piece of my soul disintegrated every time I had to play it. It made me feel ... cheap. I wanted it to die slowly and painfully.

SAF: And... ?

MKT: I completely lost my shit and stabbed it with a screwdriver. I totally blacked out, so I don't remember how many times exactly, but I think it was a lot. But don't bother looking for her...
you'll never find a woman like that.

SAF: Oh we found the body all right ...

Special Agent Forrester fumbles through his papers.

SAF: Here it is. We found the remains behind the K-Mart on Shelburne Road. It was stabbed a total of 28 times. Including ... oh, my good lord ...

seven times directly in the *asshole*.

There is no way around it, sir: These facts are quite disturbing.

So I must ask you now, Mr. Thompson, are you willfully admitting to all of these murders here today?

MKT: You're fucking right I do. And all I can say is...

      "Don't You Want Me" by Human League
         is damned lucky you caught me.

THANKS FOR THE MEMORIES.

"So I say thank you for the music,
the songs I'm singing
Thanks for the all
the joy they're bringing
Who can live without it,
I ask in all honesty
What would life be?
Without a song or a dance, what are we?
So I say thank you for the music
for giving it to me"

Thank You For The Music by ABBA
Written by Benny Andersson & Bjorn Ulvaeus
Released in 1977 on Polar

My lifetime in music and as a DJ has presented me with so many amazing rewards. From sharing the stage with some of my musical heroes (such as The Roots, A Tribe Called Quest, Morris Day & The Time, Maceo Parker, KRS-One,

Slick Rick, and Big Daddy Kane) to playing for tens of thousands of locals and tourists over the years at more than 30 local venues, my experiences have been filled with unforgettable moments. DJing has also given my wife and me numerous free trips, including one to Mexico while first dating and the first half of our honeymoon to Chicago just days after we were married. It was on that trip that I was forced to not only challenge myeslf as a DJ but to stand back and take time to appreciate all that playing music has brought to me.

It was in October of 2011. An old friend of mine was getting married in Chicago the week after our wedding and asked me to DJ her reception. In exchange, she flew us both out there and put us up in a beautiful suite for the week. Neither my wife, Emilie, nor I had ever been to Chicago, so we were excited to explore the Windy City. We had an amazing week of site-seeing, amazing food, and nightlife.

The day of my friend's wedding arrived, and I began to set up my equipment to play for the 200 guests at the exquisite ballroom they had reserved. Prior to leaving, I had organized all of the music that she wanted to add to the list of standards that I always had ready. I packed up all her requests and all of my system units and felt 100 percent prepared.

As I was setting everything up the day of, I panicked as I realized that I had brought everything *except* the standards I normally play (which were approximately 70 percent of the entire playlist for the evening)! As the guests were beginning to arrive, I began sweating like a coal miner. I realized I had about an hour and a half of music for a five-hour party. Then, as I was about to throw up in a flower vase, I remembered that I had put the missing playlists on my phone! I had a cord to plug my phone into my mixer and spent the next five hours nervously transitioning from my iphone to the CD deck and back again. I had never been so nervous but — somehow, someway — pulled off the event so smoothly that the only ones who knew were my wife and I. To this day, my friend who hired me has no idea — until she reads it here.

That moment made me step back and take stock in just what DJing had brought to my life. Memories. Moments. Material things. Motivation. A marriage. A beautiful home. And the ability to handle stressful situations with calm and reasoning. Skills that have helped me in many facets of my life to date. Certain aspects (or people) may annoy me at times; however, I'm truly grateful for all of it: the good, the bad and the ugly.

It all made me who (and what) I am today.

So allow me to say this:

Thank you, music.

BROKEN HEARTED.

"Be still my beating heart
You must learn to stand your ground
It's not healthy to run at this pace
The blood runs so red to my face
I've been to every single book I know
To soothe the thoughts that plague me so

Stop before you start
Be still my beating heart"

Be Still My Beating Heart by Sting
Written by Sting
Released in 1987 on A&M

In late 2003, my weight had ballooned to 435 pounds. I was suffering from diabetes and sleep apnea. It was a much too regular occurrence for me to run to the store and come home with the following: a large turkey and cheese sub (with extra mayo), a large bag of chips, some dip for said chips, a two-liter bottle of Mountain Dew, and a Snickers bar. Just for lunch.

My years of traveling in the band had done wonders to strengthen my gas station diet. And it was all about to catch up with me.

December 5, 2003. I was feeling extremely fatigued — like, no matter what I did, I couldn't catch up. The day before, I had slept for 20 hours, waking only to eat and piss. Yet I still felt exhausted. I remember coming back to my apartment that morning after an errand. I looked at the steep flight of stairs that led up to my apartment door and thought, *Maybe I'll just sit here for a second before I make this trek.* I wasn't putting one and two together, but something was terribly wrong with me for needing to rest before I could climb 18 stairs.

I was so weak, I started to doze off as I sat there. Someone opened the door and startled me awake. It was my friend (whom I call Poptart) who worked just two buildings down and wanted to check in on me. She could tell I was feeling weak and began asking me questions. After a few of my answers left her skeptical, she demanded that I let her drive me to the hospital. She kept telling me how green my face and skin looked and how it was scaring her.

When we got to the hospital, as is typical, we sat in the waiting room for a long time. But, as the minutes turned into an hour plus, Poptart started to freak out as she noticed my condition worsening.

It was then that she began to make some serious noise, demanding that I receive some kind of attention.
Her efforts were rewarded with a nurse coming by soon thereafter and wheeling me into a room. As the nurse asked me a few questions, she began to take my vital signals. Her face dropped, and, before I knew what was happening, I was rushed by two male nurses into an operating room where chaos erupted. Two doctors came running in and were yelling orders. As I heard one of them bark, "He's going into failure," I passed out.

When I came to approximately 40 minutes later, I was disorientated and scared. When the dust had settled, my doctor returned and rolled his chair next to my bed.
I was not prepared to hear what he was about to tell me.

"Mr. Thompson, when you arrived here today, your heart was enlarged by more than twice its normal size and was beating at around 195 beats per minute. A normal resting heart rate is between 60-80 BPMs. Your heart was quite literally about to explode in your chest. In fact, when you passed out, your heart completely stopped for about 35 seconds. We had to shock it back into regular rhythm with a defibrillator. You suffered what is called congestive heart failure and you are extremely lucky that you are still here with us. But the good news is, today is the day we begin to change your life for the better."

He laid out a plan for me that included an instant and strict diet and a plan to have gastric bypass surgery performed within 90 days. He informed me that my body was simply putting too much stress on my heart and, unless I began to lose weight immediately, I would be dead within a year. I was 33 years old.

Over the course of the next three nights I spent in that hospital bed, a lot of my time was focused on analyzing my life as a whole up to that point. I had enjoyed some amazing career successes, yet I found myself reminiscing about those individuals that I had made angry or upset. Ex-girlfriends, old friends, and bandmates — anyone and everyone I had ever stopped interacting with on bad (or unfinished) terms. I wrote all of their names down on a list and, one by one, from that hospital room, called them and apologized. Some I told about my heart failure, some I didn't. I just didn't want a second chance to be in vain.

I had the surgery soon afterwards and ended up losing almost 230 pounds. I was blessed, and all I wanted to do was take advantage of this life do-over and try to keep this state of mind every day.

Poptart, I will obviously never be able to thank you enough for literally saving my life, but I will always remember that you did. Just know you are my angel and forever will be.

And to you, the reader, if you pull nothing else from this book, please take this message with you:

Life is fucking short. Don't put *it* off.

Whatever *it* is you've been thinking about doing ... *do it*.

Don't do it for someone *else*. Do it for you.

So you truly have **no regrets**.

REALITY BITES.

"Back to life,
back to the present time,
back from a fantasy
Yeah tell me now, take the initiative,
I'll leave it in your hands
until you're ready

Back to life
back to the day we have
Let's end this foolish game
Hear me out, don't let me waste away
Make up your mind
so I know where I stand"

Back To Reality (However Do You Want Me) by Soul II Soul
Written by Jazzie B, Caron Wheeler, Nellie Hooper, Simon Law
Released in 1989 on Virgin

I don't watch a lot of TV. In fact, beyond series television like *Boardwalk Empire*, *Shameless*, *Ray Donovan*, and *Breaking Bad*, the only other TV I regularly watch is sports and the rarely spoken of "family secret."

But therapy only works if you admit to your addictions, so please allow me to drag the skeleton out of my overly cluttered closet.

It is my attraction to, and affection for, bad reality TV.

I don't mean *Survivor* or *The Apprentice*. I mean bad reality TV, like *Mob Wives*, *G's to Gents*, and (gulp) *Tool Academy*. I understand that I'm most likely losing self-respect, brain cells, and my grasp of proper manners by watching these atrocities. There's just something about people who are completely willing to give up their privacy for the purpose of gaining an audience that intrigues me.
I guess that I, somewhat sadly, enjoy the highly questionable (and non-scripted?) nonsense of it all.
Add in the naughty feeling I get while watching.

I can't help it. I simply like it way too much.

As I entered my second decade of '80s night, I began to envision the possibilities of sharing the debauchery that played out in front of me every week. Imagine if every Saturday night,

VH1 cameras and crew came in and chose three sets of couples to mic up and follow around for that episode of the newest reality show: *Instant Vintage*.

The first couple would be an older married couple, which still likes to party but has been together for some time. The focus on the two of them would be the core of their relationship, their connection to this era's music and the effects that the night's drinks would take on their demeanors.

The second couple would be either of the following: 1) a couple on their first or second date ever; or 2) a couple that have wanted to hook-up for a while but haven't linked up until this actual night. The focus on these two would be the awkwardness of their inexperience together and the manner in which their evening, and chance of leaving together, plays out.

And the third couple would be a gay couple (either men or women). As Burlington recently legalized same-sex marriage, the city has seeing a boom in sexual experimentation and freedom of choice. The focus on these two would revolve around the chances of this connection being a true love match or an impulsive yet singular moment in time.

As the series would progress, we could combine new characters weekly while revisiting previous couples for relationship updates. Some of the club's bartenders and bouncers could be comic relief, and I would be the host and voice behind the drama (a fat-ass Ryan Seacrest).

I really believe it would be a hit. A series that would show the participants in weekend mode: throwing back drinks, letting loose, and looking for some action. In my twisted mind, I see the show as a hodgepodge of previously seen bad TV (kind of a best-of-the-worst, if you will).

Kind of like a:
Real World

x

Big Brother

x

Flavor Of Love

x

Cheaters.

Imagine all the juicy possibilities....

DO-IT-YOURSELF PROJECT.

*"I close my eyes and see you before me
Think I would die if you were to ignore me
A fool could see just how much I adore you
I'd get down on my knees, I'd do anything for you*

*I don't want anybody else
When I think about you, I touch myself
Ooh, I don't want anybody else
Oh no, oh no, oh no"*

I Touch Myself by Divinyls
Written by Christina Amphlett, Tom Kelly, Mark McEntee, Billy Steinberg
Released in 1989 on Virgin

From the perch atop my elevated DJ booth at Club Metronome, I'm able to witness quite a bit. From rhythm-challenged dancing and couples arguing to drunken patrons and low-cut tops revealing way too cleavage, I have seen it all.

However, one of my favorite activities while spinning has, without a doubt, become watching young adults clumsily attempt one of America's favorite pastimes: the hook-up. Whether it's a girl pursuing a boy, a boy chasing a girl, or a same-sex scenario, it's often simultaneously uncomfortable and entertaining to witness.

For the last few years, I've followed the repeated weekly failings of one particular gentleman. He stands about 5'9", is around 30 years old, and, while not ugly, is also not someone you would describe as handsome. He just *is*. He wears his receding hair in a ponytail and shuffles around the club every week on a determined mission. That mission is to find a ladyfriend. And, from my view, that is the only criterion – that his conquest be a woman. Tall, short, skinny, fat, younger, older — it really doesn't matter to this guy. He just keeps on trying and keeps on getting rejected. But there are two things he doesn't do:

    1. He doesn't drink. Only water. I'm assuming this is to keep his "game" sharp.

    2. He never ever quits. Rejection? Just a speed bump on his way to the next target: the next closest female in the building.

Well, one night a few years back, the club was quite full, and our hero arrived to begin his regular round of rejections. I witnessed a few early fails but eventually noticed him behind me, against the windows, striking up what appeared to be a somewhat successful conversation with a cute girl in her mid-20s. She seemed genuinely interested — laughing at his jokes and lightly touching his arm (a universal sign for "I accept your advances"). As the night continued, I spotted them dancing together and getting closer. I was genuinely excited for the guy and remember thinking: He has a real shot here.

As the clock neared 1:30 a.m., I again spotted the couple dancing, and, this time, they were in full embrace and locked in a kiss. While happy for the guy, I was simultaneously hoping that he wouldn't find a way to fuck up a seemingly sure thing. And, then, he somehow did.

While grinding on the dance floor, he whispered in his partner's ear, and she suddenly pulled back. Whatever he uttered made her instantly leery of him and his intentions. She quickly said something back, turned, and slid away towards the ladies room. Despite her reaction, he didn't seem to think he had hurt his chances at all and, in fact, stood grinning like he knew he was actually (and finally) going to get laid.

But, as I finished my last song and the club began to empty out, I saw him wandering and searching for her.
I assumed that she had snuck out of the venue when she went to the "bathroom." As more people were exiting, the guy became more frantic in his search for her.

I shut down the amps and packed up my equipment. Neither he nor she were anywhere to be found. I felt bad for him as I headed out to my car in the back alley. I thought to myself, *That poor guy came so close to actually having sex with a partner tonight.* I tossed my equipment in the back of my rig and jumped in the driver's seat to head home.

As I flipped on my headlights, I saw him. He was leaning up against the wall in the back corner, and he was pumping gas. And by pumping gas I mean he was jerking off — really, really hard. One of his shoes was kicked off, his foot was bare, and in his left hand he held his removed sock (the target, I assumed, for his soon-to-be-released nut pudding). His eyes were closed and his head was bobbing back and forth, so he didn't even notice my headlights were on him like a stage spotlight. I finally tapped my horn in unison with his jerking rhythm (a straight DJ move). It must have startled him because he came on himself. He then turned, grabbed his shoe, and ran down the alley.

I've never seen him at the club again.

But he did leave his sock behind.

MOMMA'S BOY.

"Let us die young or let us live forever
We don't have the power
but we never say never
Sitting in a sandpit, life is a short trip
The music's for the sad men

Forever young, I want to be forever young
Do you really want to live forever,
forever and ever?

Forever young, I want to be forever young
Do you really want to live forever,
forever and ever?"

Forever Young by Alphaville
Written by Bernhard Lloyd, Marian Gold, Frank Mertens
Released in 1984 on WEA

My mother's first heart attack was in 1996.

I was on the road with my band, Belizbeha. I remember so clearly the phone call I received during sound check for that evening's show and how it completely rocked my world, shattering my focus and *need* to play music that day. All I wanted to do was jump on a plane and fly home, but, after talking to my sister and realizing the worst of it was behind us (and that Mom was going to be okay), I stayed where I was.

One thing I'm not at all afraid to admit: I grew up as, and always will be, a Momma's Boy. My mom was my biggest supporter and truly one of my very best friends in this big, cruel world. Her ability to listen was amazing but came in second only to her gift of being able to offer the exact words of positive-thinking advice I needed to hear at the perfect moment in my conversations with her. She was compassionate, caring, generous, and thoughtful — all qualities I strive to embody more fully every day.

I owe a lot of my successes in life to her and her steadfast advice to always "set that goal and go get it." Take this book, for example. When I told my wife that I was going to write it when the idea first came to me, she replied, "But you've never written a book." My mom's response? "I know you will, and I can't wait to read it."

She made it seem so simple to set your sights on something and just go knock it out. Easy peasy.

Over the course of the next seven years after that close call while I was on tour with Belizbeha, my mom had *four* more heart attacks. After each one, my family all experienced the following emotions (in order):

1. Relief: that this one had not finally killed her.

2. Reflection: on our lives with her to that point.

3. Gratitude: that she was still here and with us.

4. Appreciation: for whatever time we had left with her.

It felt as though we were given a gift of more time with her (especially after the fifth heart attack), when the reality was that she probably shouldn't have still been alive. Being so blessed, we vowed to never take a single second of this extra time for granted. I personally spoiled her every chance I got. Lunches, dinners, gifts, cards, messages — anything I could do to make her feel as loved as she made me feel every day.

Flash forward 10 years to February 26, 2013.

It was around 3 a.m, when the phone call came. My sister was on the line, telling me that my mom was unresponsive at my parents' home and that I should immediately head down there.

At first, I tried to convince myself that maybe she had a stroke and was going to be okay. But, as the seconds passed, I knew in my gut *this was it*. She was gone. I cried like I had never cried before.

I somehow got myself together enough to begin the 40-minute drive to Bristol. I remember that it was much warmer than usual for that time of year and, because of this, was extremely foggy. The fog was so thick that I could only see about 20 feet out in front of me. As I carefully and slowly drove through the thick mist in silence, I sobbed and thought about my mother and her life. The fog made the experience feel so surreal, as if I was floating on a cloud. It was almost like I was ascending to heaven to meet my mother at the gates. The flood of emotions welling in me, combined with the noise from the rotation of the tires against the road, made me start to freak out. So, to combat the sounds of silence, I reached over and clicked on the radio. As I drove through the town of Monkton, the signal was weak. I hit scan and, as the radio began to scroll through the possible FM stations, I drifted off in thought. Over and over again the scan rolled through the dial trying to find a station as I reminisced and bawled.

As the fog seemed to get even thicker, the scan landed on a faint signal. Driving up a steep hill, the signal strengthened, and I could hear the song.

It was "Forever Young" by Alphaville.

> *"It's so hard to get old without a cause*
> *I don't want to perish like a fading horse*
> *Youth's like diamonds in the sun*
> *And diamonds are forever*
>
> *So many adventures couldn't happen today*
> *So many songs we forgot to play*
> *So many dreams swinging out of the blue*
> *We let them come true."*

Memories swarmed my mind, and it was at least a mile before I realized that I was singing along to the eerily relevant and timely lyrics. It sent a chill down my spine as I grasped the entirety of the moment. And then, thanks to this amazing song, it was as though I ascended to a strange state of clarity. Almost a feeling of peaceful acceptance.

I still miss my Momma every single day.

I miss her words of encouragement, her unwavering ability to give unconditionally, and her endless love of family.

She's missed by so many that she touched in this physical world, but her spirit is always around me and will be until we someday meet again.

Thank you, Marielana "Lana" Rose Thompson.

For your love, support, and spirit.

SHORT CUTS.

"Another Saturday, another date
She would be ready but she always makes him wait
In the hallway, in anticipation
He didn't know the night would end up in frustration
He'd end up blowing all his wages for the week
All for a cuddle and a peck on the cheek

Come dancing, just like the palais on a Saturday
And all her friends will come dancing
Where the big bands used to play"

Come Dancing by The Kinks
Written by Ray Davies
Released in 1982 on Arista

The next few pages contain some quick takes on some of the more memorable patrons who have left their stains on my brain:

"She's a very kinky girl
The kind you don't take home to mother
She will never let your spirits down
Once you get her off the street
She's a super freak, super freak
She's super-freaky, yow!"

Super Freak by Rick James
Written by Rick James, Alonzo Miller
Released in 1981 on Gordy

There was a woman who frequented Metronome for a few years whom we all simply knew as "The Predator." She was in her mid-50s and had approximately 30 percent of her teeth left. She wore way too much cheap perfume and loved to sport ribbed turtlenecks that were a size and half too small. If I could choose one word to describe her it would be *relentless*. She was like a government-built terminator robot designed for one mission: to hit on human beings. She would scan the room with her sex-o-laser, and, when her target was locked in, she would proceed to attack mode.

Boys, girls, gay, straight, and anything and everything in between. She had no preference or type.

I would watch as she would slither up to an unsuspecting guy at the bar and lean right in for the kill. As he realized her age, smell and/or missing tooth total, he would back-pedal and somehow escape. She would then turn to, literally, whatever human being (not with a partner) was next closest, and they instantly became the subsequent prey. She'd relentlessly move from male to female, rejection to denial, for a solid two to three hours, then leave. Then she'd return the following week for more Saturday evening snubs. One week, after her regular failures, she just disappeared.

Flash forward a few years later to when my wife and I bought our home just outside of town, I went to our now local grocery store to buy some food. Imagine my surprise when I got to the express aisle and recognized the cashier.

That's right: "The Predator."

She eye-balled me up and down as she rang up my purchases. When I turned to grab my bag, she lightly touched my hand, gave me a toothless grin and, under her cigarette-scented breath, gruffly purred:

"I'm off at 9 tonight, sweetie."

"You come on with it, come on
You don't fight fair
That's okay, see if I care
Knock me down, it's all in vain
I get right back on my feet again

Hit me with your best shot
Why don't you hit me with your best shot
Hit me with your best shot
Fire away"

Hit Me With Your Best Shot by Pat Benatar
Written by Eddie Schwartz
Released in 1980 on Chrysalis

After my succesful gastric bypass surgery and dramatic weight loss, I found a new addiction: *women*. It's amazing the effect that losing over 200 pounds can have on your libido (for a number of reasons). One, women you know are impressed and compliment you. Two, women you don't know finally notice you. And three, you can finally see your dick again.

The combination of these factors led to my slutty phase,

during which I slept with a bunch of women just because I could. I was always safe, but I sometimes slept with someone simply because I was so thirsty for something to drink.

One girl in particular though was the reality check I needed to wake up from this promiscuous period and slow my roll. For the purpose of this story, I'll call her Rocky.

Rocky was an older divorced mom who was three things that made her a prime target for me at this time: She was a semi-regular at Metronome, she was sexy as hell, and she was a pretty big drunk. Late one Saturday just after closing, I literally bumped into her on my way out of the club. We laughed about it and made small talk, and then she placed her hand on my shoulder and asked, "So, where are you taking me right now?" I only lived two blocks away and was so confident at the time that my only response, as I took her by the hand and headed home, was, "To someplace *you've* never been."

We entered my apartment, and she excused herself to the restroom. I poured us each a strong drink, but we never touched them. She came out of the bathroom buck-ass naked and led me straight to my bed. We immedietly began having sex. Things are off to a good start, right? Wrong.

It was beyond awkward.

She kept pushing me to be rougher, demanding that I smack her on the ass. I obliged, leaving big, red hand marks. But she was far from satisfied and chided me for not slapping her harder. Then she asked me to pull her hair — to the point of pulling some out. I was trying my best to keep her happy but felt strange about the direction in which this all seemed to be headed.

Then things got really weird. She slid underneath me, and, as we started having missionary sex, she grunted, "Slap my titties!" in a low, gravelly voice that sounded like Vin Diesel. I lightly whacked the side of her bossom. She became more agitated. "No, you fucking pussy, punch me in the tits!"

I stopped. I stood up, picked up her clothes, and brought them over to my front door. I opened the door and placed her clothes in a heap outside on the hallway floor. I walked back over to the bed. I took her by the hand and led her from the bedroom to the front door, outside into the empty hallway and left her standing there naked with her clothes. Then I turned and re-entered my apartment. I said, "Goodnight, weirdo" and shut the door. I latched my lock and went to bed.

She didn't say a single word.

Then I jerked off. Sorry, I'm a lover, not a fighter.

I'll never hear the saying "I can't wait to *hit* that" the same way again.

"I can see it in your eyes
I can see it in your smile
You're all I've ever wanted
And my arms are open wide
Cause you know just what to say
And you know just what to do

Hello. Is it me your looking for?"

Hello by Lionel Richie
Written by Lionel Richie
Released in 1984 on Motown

When I was still spinning from my booth behind the stage at Metronome, I had a hard time seeing people's faces out of my 2" x 3' peephole. One particular friend made that mystery a memory for life one evening.

One of my friends from home was a tall, tomboyish girl whom I'll call DeeDee. That's because she had some amazing triple-D titties. And she loved to show them: to friends and strangers alike. She would always show up at '80s night plastered and (in her likable way) annoy me with her requests.

One night she was trying to get to me through the window but was blocked by two young ladies who were requesting songs of their own.
I could see her behind them — anxious and agitated. The longer these two took with me, the more DeeDee began to dance in place like she had to pee really bad.

Then it happened.

As I was finishing speaking with these two innocent bystanders, DeeDee slipped her left boob out of her worn-out tank top and was waving it near the bottom of the window. The two ladies either noticed and/or felt pushed out of the way and turned to leave. I laughed at DeeDee's sand dollar areola and looked away to focus on mixing in the next song.

When I looked back up, Not only was DeeDee's boob now fully in the window, but she had attached a wooden clothespin to the nipple, and she was shaking the enormous breast back and forth to the tempo of the beat. The clothespin swung wildly back and forth, and she was shaking it so violently (and her booby was so ridiculously large) that the wood was clicking against the top and bottom of the window. She yelled at me to "Lick it!".

So I leaned forward, removed the clothespin, and sucked the nip hard for 3 to 4 seconds. She shrieked a little in enjoyment and cuffed me in the side of the face with the bouncing bossom.

Then she left.

#boob-tease.

*Note from my editor regarding this story:

What's in this story for me? You have a friend from home with big tits, and you sucked them. That's the story? I was a little creeped out by this, but, then, I may not be your core audience.

On the other hand, if you ever wake up one day and realize that I am your core audience, you've made a seriously wrong turn in life and should probably kill yourself.

"We can dance if we want to
We can leave your friends behind
Cause your friends don't dance
and if they don't dance
Well, they're no friends of mine

We can dance, we can dance
Everybody look at your hands
We can dance, we can dance
Everybody's taking the chance
Safety dance"

Safety Dance by Men Without Hats
Written by Ivan Doroschuk
Released in 1983 on GMC/Virgin

Any time you have a night that revolves around the familiarity of huge retro hits, you are completely unable to escape two consequences: 1) A combination of both amazingly awkward and horribly bad dancing and 2) the ultimate in lip-syncing. The dancing is almost too bad to be real. It's like they are trying to dance off beat, yet their serious facial expressions let you know they're all in.

The lip-syncing is where the real rock stars shine. And Metronome has a stage where the uninhibited (read as: drunk) can step up to the spotlight and become their favorite hero for three epic minutes.

Out of the thousands of patrons who have graced the club with their presence over the years, I can think of two who have earned the crown as champs. The first is the young fellow who has been a regular to that stage over the last three years or so. He's my choice as dance champion for his plus/minus ratio. His plus is his "running man," which is one of the best I have ever witnessed (and, believe me, I have seen some "running man" in my day). His minus is the sum total of the rest of his dance moves combined. As good as he is at the running man, he's at least twice as bad at everything else. So, the combination is a majestic car wreck from which you can not turn away. I thank him from the bottom of my heart for the hours of entertainment with which he has blessed us.

The second champ is the trucker-hat-wearing regular (from around 2005-2008) who *owned* the stage when it came to lip-syncing '80s rock.

"Living On A Prayer"?
"Shook Me All Night Long"?
"Sweet Child O' Mine"?

This fucker would make you feel like not only was he singing (or screaming) every word *to* you, but that he had also personally *lived* each story and **hand-written** the words himself. He ruled our little '80s night stage with the fierceness of his passion, which both fascinated and frightened me (along with most of the female patrons he sang in the faces of each week).

*"Don't switch the blade on the guy in shades;
oh no
Don't masquerade with the guy in shades;
(oh no) (I can't believe it)
You got it made with the guy in shades; oh no*

*I wear my sunglasses at night
So I can, So I can
Forget my name while you collect your claim
And I wear my sunglasses at night
So I can, So I can
See the light that's right before my eyes"*

Sunglasses At Night by Corey Hart
Written by Corey Hart
Released in 1984 on EMI

One of my strict rules for doing a five-hour set is to try my hardest *never* to repeat a song within a night. While there may be reasons to do so, I generally believe in trying my darndest not to. But one time, around three or four years into my Retronome residency, I was given 150 reasons to reconsider my rule.

Over the years, multiple patrons have uttered the words, "If you play this song next, I'm definitely getting laid." Well, I tend to think if it comes down to the '80s DJ playing a song for you or not, your chances of having sex are most likely slim. But, depending on my mood and who is asking, I sometimes like to participate in the experiment (even if only to prove them wrong). So, nearing the end of a packed-full fall evening, a very drunken gentleman in his late 30s approached the booth and tried this very lame attempt. He desperately wanted to hear "Sunglasses At Night" by Corey Hart. I was agitated by his approach (and his level of intoxication) so I was happy to be able to reply with my rule: "No, sir, I'm sorry. I already played that one earlier and really don't play songs twice in a night."

He scoffed and slurred, "Everything has a price, bucko."

I agreed with him but quickly let him know that my prices were steep (as I mostly just wanted him to leave me alone).

He said, "Name it".

I normally tell people 10 or 20 bucks for a quicker request, but I saw a golden opportunity here. I said, "One-hundred bucks to play it and one-fifty to play it right now. Period."

He dug in his pockets, turned, and yelled at a buddy nearby. Between the two of them, they came up with seven crumpled $20s and a $10 and tossed them at me. I scooped them up and immediately stopped the song playing and dropped his purchased jam. I then watched as his love interest sprinted across the floor, dove into his arms, and wrapped her legs around him. (Did I mention they both pulled out and slipped on cheap imitation Ray-Bans?)

When the song ended, she jogged over to my window and slurred, "You just got this guy some pussy."

Sliding the money into my pocket, I never felt more like a pimp in my entire life.

Transaction completed.

"So we journeyed to her house
One thing led to another
I keyed the door, I cold hit the floor
Looked up and it was her mother

I didn't know what to say
I was hanging by a string
She said, "Hey, you two, I was once like you
And I liked to do the wild thing"

Wild Thing by Tone Loc
Written by Young MC
Released in 1988 on Delicious Vinyl

I have wished thousands of club-goers happy birthdays over the years, but one particular birthday will forever be entrenched in my mind.

One night, I was approached by a set of cute identical twin girls in their early 20s. They politely asked me asked me if I could wish their great-grandmother a happy birthday. I chuckled and told them I could, but that I generally did birthday shout-outs to those who were presently *in* the club. They excitedly shrieked, "She is!"

Now totally curious, I asked where. They pointed to the bar where their mother, grandmother, and great-grandmother stood ordering shots. They said her name was Lucille and that she'd turned 83 that day! I thought for a moment and then told them that I didn't think I had ever wished anyone over the age of 60 a happy birthday there, so I wanted to play her favorite '80s songs for her. They excitedly scampered to tell her and brought her back over to me.

"Happy Birthday, Miss Lucille! Those shots are on me!

What song can I play you for your birthday, ma'am?"

She gave me a mischievous grin, smacked my ass as hard as she could with her boney little hand, and announced, "Gimme some Wild Thing!"

"'Wild Thing,' huh?" I asked.

"You know it, honey! I love me some Tone-fucking-Loc."

"Ain't nothin' gonna to break my stride
Nobody's gonna slow me down, oh-no
I got to keep on movin'
Ain't nothin' gonna break my stride
I'm running and I won't touch ground
Oh-no, I got to keep on movin'"

Break My Stride by Matthew Wilder
Written by Matthew Wilder, Greg Prestopino
Released in 1983 on Private-I

One of the perks of being a DJ is being able to drink while you work. When you are allowed to drink while you work, that means you can get loaded with your friends who come to dance while you spin. Since I only lived about a block and a half away from the club for the first 11 years of my Metronome gig — a short walk (or stumble) — I had some real sloppy finishes.

One of my very good friends, Eleanor (or Nellie), also lived close by and also enjoyed getting drunk and stumbling home. When it came to drinking, Nellie had a strong *work ethic*. The job wasn't done until she said it was, and she (quite often) was the cheerleader for that ever-destructive last round.

You know, the one you always wish you hadn't ordered when you're super hungover at around 10:30 Sunday morning? The completely unnecessary round? Yeah, that was her favorite. And those last rounds led her to one of two situations: the ill-timed and questionable makeout session with a stranger or the imminent loss of one her flip-flops.

Yup, that's what I said. Nellie was famous for flicking off her left flip-flop in a drunken hissy fit. While this could be funny on its own, what was even more hilarious was that she'd amazingly stroll outside the next day to find the missing shoe — right where she'd left it. She never even realized she was missing the thing until she went to slide them on the next morning.

But absolutely best of all is that (to date), Nellie has accomplished this loss and recovery mission *three* times successfully.

She recently moved out of the downtown area and now has to take a cab home, so only time will tell if the local cab companies help her continue her *reunions*.

*"Everybody was Kung Fu fighting
Those kids were fast as lightning
In fact it was a little bit fright'ning
But they did it with expert timing."*

Kung Fu Fighting by Carl Douglas
Written by Carl Douglas, Biddu Appaiah
Released in 1974 on 20th Century Fox

One of my other semi-regular DJ gigs in town is at a venue called Halflounge Speakeasy. It's a small, hip spot that reaches capacity at about 50 souls, but I enjoyed it because I wasn't restricted by a certain format and could play whatever I wanted. One hot summer night, there were around 30 people lounging about when *she* entered.

She was a 25- to 30-year-old hippie who (from first view) we all knew was on some combination of serious drugs. She entered the room with face-high karate kicks-slash-dance moves. It was almost as if she were battling an army of invisible bad guys — but to the beat. She proceeded to move some chairs out of the way so she had more room to fight her make believe criminals. But just then, she peeled off her long sleeve shirt to unleash her furry pits and *the odor*.

Now, when I say odor, I'm not talking about a perfume or body spray. The entire room suddenly smelled as though a rat had died and been shit upon. I looked around the room. Patrons' eyes watered as they pinpointed the source. Meanwhile, the dancer continued to kung fu fight her imaginary battle. Some people were so overtaken by the smell that they literally had to leave. I wished I could've left as well. Eventually, the bouncer had to ask her to move along, ignoring the smell issue by blaming it on her dangerous and risky high kicks.

I'll never forget the beauty of her Bruce Lee dance moves or the potent power of her Pigpen arm pits.

"Oh baby, I'll take you down, I'll take you down
Where no one's ever gone before
And if you want more, if you want more, more, more

Jump for my love,
Jump in and feel my touch
Jump if you want to taste my kisses in the night, then
Jump, jump for my love."

Jump (For My Love) by The Pointer Sisters
Written by Stephen Mitchell, Marti Sharron, Gary Skardina
Released in 1984 on Planet

One thing I've learned for certain from the last 16 years is that gay folk love them some '80s music. From Madonna to Prince to Whitney, all the way to the ultimate gay anthem: "It's Raining Men." It's no secret: the '80s were pretty much the gayest decade. One of my all-time favorite regulars during the early years of '80s night was a short, chubby gentleman I called Theo (mainly because he looked like an overweight Theo Huxtable from *The Cosby Show*).

Theo was famous in these parts for three things:

1. He was wham-bam-flamboyantly gay and brought the party like his life depended on it.

2. He wasn't the *best* dancer you had ever laid your eyes upon, but, in his mind, he sure as shit was. He absolutely *owned* it. And...

3. He led the charge for the Soul Train line like a champ.

Now, for those who don't know, *Soul Train* was a TV show that aired from 1971-2006 and featured soul and pop music performances and some of the best dancing from the eras it spanned. A Soul Train line is two rows of people with either a single person or a couple dancing (in between) from the back to the front. It is an opportunity to showcase your best moves and really makes a party pop off. Theo had a knack for lining them up quickly, energetically leading the charge, and (most importantly), knowing when the Train had run its course for the night. Nothing worse than a Train that doesn't know when its time has passed.

I'm not positive, but I think Theo moved to Chicago in the early 2000s.

Here's what I know for certain:

I wish I knew your real name, man, and I wish you still lived here to lead the rhythmically challenged every week.

"Jammin' on the one."

Fini.

CLOSING TIME.

"You know that I've seen
too many romantic dreams
Up in lights, fallin' off the silver screen
My hearts like an open book
for the whole world to read
Sometimes, nothing keeps me
together at the seams
I'm on my way, I'm on my way
Home sweet home, tonight tonight
I'm on my way, just set me free
Home sweet home"

Home Sweet Home by Motley Crue
Written by Nikki Sixx, Vince Neil & Tommy Lee
Released in 1985 on Electra

The moment the clock strikes 2 a.m. at Club Metronome is nothing short of a trip — an alcohol-fueled climax, if you will.

It's the big reveal: that moment when the lights get flipped on and the last of the patrons experience the simultaneus emotions of excitement and disapointment as all of the secrets of the dark are set free. This sparks different reactions from the different sub-groups who've made it all the way to the end. For a few, this is a good thing. For others, its a bad thing. And, for a select number, its the worst thing imaginable. Let's break them all down, shall we?

Group 1: The Dancing Queens. For this group, the emotions lie somewhere between pissed and devastated. They are so immersed in the music and their dance moves that, when the lights come up and they realize it's time to go, they are nearly on the verge of tears. They wish with with all their might that the night would simply never end.

Group 2: The Drunkies. This group is ambivilent. They are so loaded that they don't even realize it's 2 a.m. and continue to stand at the bar with a $10 bill in their hand trying to order another round (even though the bar staff acts as though they are now invisible).

Group 3: The Never-Giver-Uppers. This small collective are the ones who've spent the night trying to keep up with their alcoholic friends, drink for drink, only to have failed. These ambitious but flawed few have stuck it out to avoid being called a "pussy" by their roomates and regret not only the last drink, but the last four.
They have also thrown-up in their mouths at least twice since 1 o'clock. They are relieved that it is finally time to leave and more than excited to scurry out the front door and devour three slices of pizza before vomiting for real.

Group 4: The Hook-Up Artists. These are the ones in full-on makeout mode in the center of the dance floor. These encounters head in one of two directions as the clock strikes 2 a.m.: 1) They leave with their new friend and go directly to either person's apartment, excited to hit the hay with a warm body at the end a cold winter's night filled with too much drinking; or, 2) the harshness of the floodlights being turned on allow them to truly see the face of their kissing buddy, bringing with it the reality of a situation that now looks quite different than it had in the dark. These are ones you see rushing out, heads down and looking like they've just seen a ghost.

And, lastly, Group 5: The Bar Staff.

The main emotions shared among the staff are bliss and gratitude. These are due to the fact that they have made it through another Saturday night, and it is now time to clean up and close shop. The marathon is over for another week and, beyond a few minor injuries, they have all (for all intensive purposes) survived.

See you all next week!

MY FINAL STAND.

"Each night I go to bed
I pray the Lord my soul to keep
No I ain't looking for forgiveness
But before I'm six foot deep
Lord, I got to ask a favor
And I'll hope you'll understand
'Cause I've lived life to the fullest
Let the boy die like a man
Staring down the bullet
Let me make my final stand

Shot down in a blaze of glory
Take me now but know the truth
I'm going out in a blaze of glory
Lord I never drew first
But I drew first blood"

Blaze Of Glory by Bon Jovi
Written by Jon Bon Jovi
Released in 1990 on Vertigo

The clock struck 1:49 a.m. late one Saturday night.

The dance floor at Metronome was packed full of sweaty, drunken dancers. From high upon my DJ booth perch, I surveyed the scene and did something I had never done before – I reached over and flipped the fader volume to off mid-song. The crowd, upset and confused by the sudden silence, turned and began to boo me viciously. "It's not 2 a.m. yet!" they yelled. "What the fuck, dude?" someone else blurted out. I calmly picked up the microphone to address the agitated crowd and declared, "It's been a great run, but it all ends here tonight." And with a dementedly evil grin, I said, "That's all, folks!"

What happened next was a surprise to everyone there except me. I reached into the waistline of my jeans and slid out a Smith & Wesson .44 Magnum pistol (an exact replica of Dirty Harry's from the movies). I casually placed the tip of the gun up under my chin, waved a last bye-bye to everyone, pulled the trigger, and blasted my brains all over the ceiling. As my instantly dead body fell in a heap to the ground, the crowd shrieked and screamed in horror and utter disbelief. Then, like in an old-time detective movie, an image of the *Burlington Free Press* newspaper appeared frantically spinning and landed face up.

The headline read:

"LOCAL DJ FINALLY LOSES IT, TAKES OWN LIFE DURING BON JOVI SONG"

And then...

I woke up — in my bed, gasping for air.

Once I gathered myself, I realized that I had dreamt the entire scenario. I nervously chuckled out loud. In my twisted little mind, I had made up an entire finale to a sad movie about the crazed DJ and his last few moments still alive.

Was it a nightmare or a wishful dream?

I'll let my shrink try to answer that one.

NEVER TEAR US APART.

"We could live
For a thousand years
But if I hurt you
I'd make wine from your tears

I told you
That we could fly
'Cause we all have wings
But some of us don't know why

I, I was standing
You were there
Two worlds collided
And they could never ever tear us apart."

Never Tear Us Apart by INXS
Written by Andrew Farriss and Michael Hutchence
Released in 1988 on Atlantic

DJ

noun

Short for disc jockey, a DJ is a person
who mixes recorded music for an audience.

To be a great DJ, one must understand that it is about
more than just being a selector of songs:

It is truly learning to understand the mood shared
by a room full of people and how to direct their emotional
state to a unified destination.

To realize this, a DJ must recognize that he or she has
the ability to impact peoples' lives spiritually and
(at least for a moment) make an entire room
fall in love:

with the music, themselves, and each other.

While there are aspects (and moments) of any job that can become annoying, I truly love being a DJ and am so thankful for all my years at Club Metronome. I have been blessed beyond belief to be the one in the driver's seat of this never-ending party. The joy I have brought to thousands of dancing locals and tourists who have passed through the 'Nome doors will always stay with me. My endless gratitude goes out to all of the
owners who have allowed me to
do my thing for coming up on two decades.

Thank You:
Nectar Rorris, Anne Rothwell, Mark Gauthier, Damon Brink, Chris Walsh, Noel Donnelly, Jason Gelrud, and Alex Budney

And to Sergei the soundman:
I still love your grumpy ass.

Love live the '80s.
May we never be torn (too far) apart.

Huge thanks go out to:

Erik Esckilsen:
For your editing prowess and your friendship.

My sister, Stephanie Larsen:
For you love, advice, support and proof reading.

Craig Mitchell:
For handing this night over to me and the years of dirty stories we've shared.

My cat, Ritchie:
For laying all over my book notes.

And last, but not least,
The Metronome Faithful:
For your devotion, emotion and constant motivation

An actual Yik Yak post.

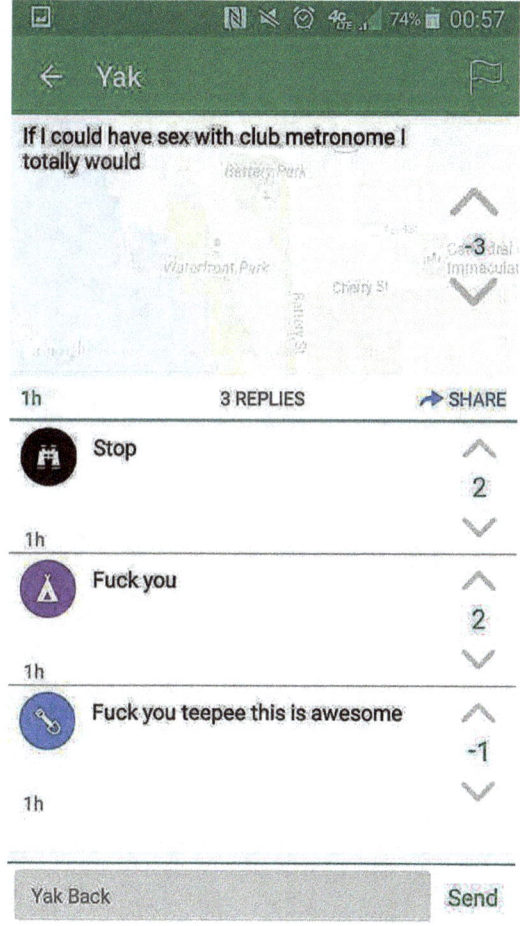

THE END.

I WAS A 400-POUND '80s DJ

Copyright 2015   Martin Kyle Thompson

ISBN 978-0-692-48071-7

All rights reserved. No part of this publication may be reproduced, stored in a retrieval system, or transmitted, in any form or by any means, electronic, mechanical, photocopying, recording, or otherwise, without the prior permission from the author.

This book is sold subject to the condition that it shall not, by trade or otherwise, be lent, re-sold, hired out or otherwise circulated without the author's prior consent in any form of binding or cover other than that in which it is published and without a similar condition including this condition being imposed on the subsequent purchaser.

www.ingramcontent.com/pod-product-compliance
Lightning Source LLC
Chambersburg PA
CBHW051943290426
44110CB00015B/2085